30 WAYS TO
MONEY IN PR

Rosters Ltd.

Other books by Luke Johnson

How To Get A Highly Paid Job In The City   £4.95

The Key To Making Money In The New Stock
Market   £5.95

The Crash Of '87 And How To Profit From It   £4.95

30 Ways To Make Money In Franchising   £4.95

30 WAYS TO MAKE MONEY IN PROPERTY

Luke Johnson
&
Ian Gill

ROSTERS LTD.

Rosters Ltd, 60 Welbeck St, London, W1.

First published in Great Britain in 1989

ISBN 0948032 43 X

Typeset in Linotron Palatino by
Rowland Phototypesetting Ltd, Bury St Edmunds, Suffolk
Printed and bound in Great Britain by
Cox and Wyman Ltd, Reading, Berks

Contents

Introduction 7

Acknowledgements 8

Why Property? 11

The Ten Golden Rules of the Property Business 15

1 Become an Estate Agent 23
2 Letting Residential Property 27
3 Buy at Auction 31
4 Raise Bank Finance 37
5 Do Your Own Surveys 41
6 Getting Planning Permission 47
7 Collect Ground Rents 49
8 Find Shop Upper Parts 53
9 Design Beautiful Interiors and Layouts 57
10 Make Finders' Fees 61
11 Buy via a Tender Offer 65
12 Sell Well 69
13 Dealing in Land 73
14 Save on Tax 79
15 Invest in Farmland 83
16 Develop Timeshare Resorts 87
17 Contrary Investment in Property 91
18 Build Hotels 95

19   Dealing in New Homes   99
20   Buying US Property   103
21   Run a Letting Agency   107
22   Choose the Right Location   111
23   Sell without an Estate Agent   115
24   Obtain a Mortgage   121
25   Buy Property on the Stock Market   125
26   Become a Builder   129
27   Get a Grant   133
28   Profit from Enterprise Zones and the BES   137
29   Enfranchise Freeholds   141
30   Raise Equity Finance   145

Glossary   149

Bibliography   157

Introduction

This book was written to help the many aspiring British property entrepreneurs. Most property books fall in to one of two categories: they are either very basic guides to house purchase for beginners, or fairly academic tomes published for qualified practising property professionals. We have tried here to present an accessible guide with an emphasis on active money-making. We have put together information unavailable from any other single source.

We don't answer *all* possible property questions, but the essential facts of the topics covered are included. As a matter of caution we would counsel readers to gain advice from other lawyers, developers, agents and architects before proceeding to invest large sums of money.

If readers have any questions or comments, they should write to the authors, care of Investors Imprint, 72 Ledbury Road, London W11 2AH.

Acknowledgements

Considerable thanks are due yet again to the ever-enthusiastic Norris. Luke is grateful to Steven S. for his property expertise and advice, and to Hugh for his bearish outlook on property.

This book is dedicated to Barbara Hunt

Why Property?

Land and property have enriched more people throughout history than any other assets. The improvement of property has built more fortunes than any other business activity, save perhaps dealing in stocks. In an island such as Britain, the supply of accommodation is scarce, and the demand for shelter more basic than any other, except food and water. Dealing in property is characterised by massive competition and by an endless pool of buyers and sellers – at the right price. Transactions tend to be few but of high value, and considerable profit can be generated by a single deal, if it is a good one.

Property development and dealing has several highly attractive features which are worth stating in simple terms.

1 You can borrow money against property: property is the finest asset against which to secure loans, despite its relative illiquidity. Banks will always accept it for borrowings up to 70% of its value, and occasionally more. There is always a market in property, so it is always possible to obtain valuations, and there is never a shortage of lenders willing to use it to guarantee an advance. Many businesses however comprise fast-depreciating plant and equipment or a high amount of intangible goodwill – lenders are frequently unhappy about extended loans with these type of assets as security.

2 Dealing in property does not have to be a full-time occupation: I know many successful developers who started with modest sums using their spare time to buy and improve houses. Today those individuals are worth millions. They have rarely had to start work before 10am, and normally wrap up their working day around 5pm.

While weekend and evening work is not unknown, it is a great rarity. A key deal, after all, can be done in just a few vital phone calls or with a simple planning application. In very few careers can one make so much money in such a short space of time.

3   Property is not a complex subject: anyone with an ounce of sense can judge a house and find out its market worth. Organising improvements to a derelict property does not require a huge level of technical skill at construction. All the necessary legal and architectural advice can easily be bought in when appropriate. And there are endless and ever growing numbers of estate agents ready to offer their views on marketing a property and finding tenants, rent reviews etc. for commercial properties. Some remarkably stupid individuals have amassed great wealth in property. Few developers have qualifications – many are from the lowliest backgrounds. They are living proof that persistence and deal-making ability are finer attributes for a developer than any degree certificate.

4   The opportunities are always there: homes, offices, shops and industrial buildings are an essential component of civilization. People are forever moving and trading their homes and places of work. The age of much of Britain's residential and commercial property stock means there will always be room to improve much accommodation. The relatively buoyant UK economy means there is a rising desire among working people to buy their own homes. Strong consumer spending encourages the retail sector, stimulating demand for shops. A recovering industrial base is increasing the requirement for factories, warehouses etc., while the powerful service sector creates an insatiable demand for office space in many locations. Large surveying practices regularly carry out research to project tenant demand for space, and most signs show the graph moving comfortably upwards. There are clearly still fortunes to be made renovating and building.

5 The satisfaction of making something: when you entirely refurbish a battered old house, the effect is hugely pleasing. Upgrading derelict property enhances the environment, and means finer accommodation has been released. There is creativity in designing a house conversion into flats so as to offer the best living space while making the maximum use of the square footage. As gentrification has spread through previous slums, such as much of Notting Hill in West London, so the area has improved immeasurably. Once you have made your mark upon a property – or an entire area – it is permanent, and will probably last more than your lifetime. It can be most fulfilling to drive past a smart parade of shops which you developed, and feel that you were ultimately responsible.

6 The risks in property are less: residential property has appreciated annually in a virtually uninterrupted trend in this country since 1945. Quite a number of developers went under in 1974 in the so-called property crash, following the secondary banking crisis, but they were invariably taking far greater risks than normal. If you are reasonably prudent, it is quite difficult to go badly wrong. While you may not make as high a return from a specific deal because building costs overran, or because the resale price was lower than expected, at the same time it takes a real amateur or a wild gambler to lose large sums of money. Compared to the risks of financial failure in conventional business enterprises, property is as safe as – well, houses! Property development and investment does not need the same level of hands-on experience and dedication that so many new businesses do.

7 Property is useful: it's difficult to justify many commercial activities except as vehicles to make someone profit. Real estate development, on the other hand, improves accommodation and can enhance the community. Capable architects can construct marvellous buildings which replace eyesores or derelict land. Such work is of benefit to the community, and a successful

13

developer can justifiably feel proud if he has been responsible for likable projects.

8 Property is accommodation and profit: a high proportion of people in Britain today are obliged to enter the property market for shelter. Once you have bought a home, you have become a property investor. The experience you acquire in so doing – and possibly if you do the place up – can serve towards a profitable sideline in property development. And you can yield better profits on your main home with some sound market knowledge and estate agency contacts – through buying in the right area for a good price. Property is such an essential asset that to avoid it is to miss out on much.

There are many other reasons why property is an interesting and profitable career, but these are the critical points. While it is possibly unlikely that you will ever build a worldwide business empire through property, the positive points are such that it makes most other businesses seem a lot of work for very little return. The following list of 30 property areas to pursue is by no means exhaustive. Each section gives the basics of a subject. You should find indications of how to take further action or find out more from each section. A few sections are primarily for bigger league investors – having perhaps £250,000 up – but most are available to average (but ambitious) wealth individuals. No section is guaranteed as to accuracy, but wherever possible facts were checked. Any one of the 30 sections could make you thousands of pounds. By diversifying across several areas, you could make £1,000,000 in a short time – with determination, intelligence, and luck. Let's hope you make it!

The Ten Golden Rules of the Property Business

1 Use the Best Advisors

Many property beginners are tempted to make use of the services of lawyers who offer cut-price conveyancing. Others feel they know enough to tackle the legalities themselves. This approach is a mistake. Few property transactions in Britain are straight-forward, thanks to a farcically complex and long-winded legal system. A good lawyer is therefore essential to guide one though the mantraps and point out the short-cuts. Try to find a solicitor who specialises in property matters, and who will give a personal and prompt service. Do not necessarily immediately plump for a smart firm based in the West End of London who charge exorbitant fees, on the other hand. Unless you undertake major deals, you will end up being palmed off with an exceedingly junior partner or articled clerk – but you will still be paying £50 or more an hour for the privilege. Ideally you should cultivate an energetic and knowledgeable character with whom you get on. While initially he may not make very much money out of you as a client, if you are successful his fees will bloom – as they should.

The same applies to architects: do not try to draw up plans yourself – they will simply be turned down by planners for consents, and builders will make a hash of the work. If you skimp on architect fees you are likely to end up with second-rate designs and lower selling prices – as well as a slower project. You must develop an able team around you who follow your instructions but guide you through technical problems. Reliability and swiftness are paramount traits which all sound professional advisors should possess.

2 Know Your Areas and Values

Rich developers tend to focus on certain patches of a particular city or region and gain a vast understanding of that market. They often acquire experience of every street, the entire local planning department, and all the agents – both the clever and incompetent ones. They build a reputation for being active in the area, and so deals will be brought to them. While they would always confirm valuations on sites where necessary, they store up such a bank of values of local deals done that when they are offered something they know if it's cheap or not. Worthwhile builders and talented selling agents will also be among their acquaintances, so that they can call up all the help required to process a deal at the drop of a hat.

If you rove around different districts in search of bargains, you will end up buying fag-ends after all the local spivs have turned them. Agents and builders and other developers will rip you off, since you are a new boy in town with no reputation and innocence glittering in your eyes. You will believe the wrong agent when he gives you inflated resale values and end up dropping money on a stumer deal. Stick to a patch you believe has potential and give it time and attention and you will reap rewards.

3 Make Friends with the Agents

Estate agents are the source of virtually all deals. Without their leads and sales pitches, you would hear of nothing. Through their endless particulars, boards, phone calls and press adverts, they communicate to the world at large about what can be bought. You must assiduously become a welcome customer of several prominent local agents if you are to be a success. Perhaps just one excellent contact can supply enough deals – but you must be top of his list, and he must be capable. Whether it takes lavish lunches or cash bribes, you must try to be the developer client who stands out and deserves the first call when the magic deal arrives. While on the surface many agents can seem brittle and smarmy, they are also keen to make money and get ahead. You can help them achieve that aim. You can also be just that bit more friendly than the next would-be developer. One way of gaining a fan club among agents is to act swiftly and decisively. That means that you do not back out of deals all the time after dithering for a month. The conveyancing system allows one to do this on many UK property transactions – but it doesn't endear you to the introducing agent and it means you won't make money (even if you don't lose any!).

Some developers nurture joint ventures with agents, whereby the agent has a carried interest in any deals he introduces – at no cost to him. This gives the agent plenty of motivation and fully involves him in the deals. But make sure any such arrangement is permitted by the firm he works for. A further twist pioneered by agents in recent years is to establish an estate agent's shop as a front to find deals and support a deal-finding agent. With the right individual this type of set-up can work, but few genuine vendors will be fooled if the agency business itself is a pure front for a deal-doing operation.

4   Don't Fall in Love with Your Properties

Buildings can be elegant things, and simply possessing them can feel grand. However, there is always an attractive selling price for any deal – make sure you take the money if you are offered it. The multitude of developers around, especially in the South-East, means mugs with money walk the streets just waiting to over-pay. Even if you only exchanged on some premises the day before receiving the right offer – take it. Another, higher offer may never come, and the development proceeds if you undertake the project may disappoint. Even a £10,000 turn on a £200,000 project is attractive if the effort and expense involved are tiny and there are risks attached to going through with the deal yourself. Some of the most successful major property companies around, such as Mountleigh and City Merchant Developers, will wheel and deal as much as they develop. All property is trading stock and should be treated as such.

5 Look at Propositions from All Sources

One of the attractive – and scary – features of the property game is that you never know when the next deal might crop up – and you never know from where it might come. This means a developer's door must always be open, and a dealer must always be willing to consider a deal – from no matter what direction. Don't simply dismiss a property because it is being offered by a sharp fellow – perhaps he's made a mistake this time. Listen to an agent's offerings, even if they've been on his books for months and he's never found anything of merit before – this may be the great bargain. Keep you eyes peeled for interesting estate agent's boards, and scrutinise the trade press and newspaper display and classified adverts for deals.

6 Create Your Own Deals

One of the most successful developers I've ever met would often stop in a likely-looking street and start knocking on doors asking if the occupants wanted to sell. Occasionally the reply was abusive, but from time to time it led to something. This was a highly practical demonstration of how no developer should sit back and wait for the deals to flow in: he should be constantly out there hustling and looking for angles. Harry Hyams, possibly one of the most successful post-war developers, was never to be found in his offices at his estate agency employers – he was always out looking for deals. If you have a flair for spotting ripe properties, and the energy to

18

follow up leads, you will certainly come across better deals than your rival who relies entirely on agents contacting him.

Creating your own deals means chasing possibilities hard if you see them. Many properties have hidden ownership and complex histories, or are entangled in legal hogwash. A fair degree of persistence is need to coax certain sellers and to assemble interesting development blocks – look how long Mr Palumbo took to assemble the Mansion House project! Likewise being patient in finding or evicting tenants is an invaluable trait. You should always be thinking up new ideas to find properties – try obtaining a list from the council of all houses with closing orders, and circularising them with letters asking if they will sell – or approach the biggest local quarrying firm to see whether they have land to offload. Attempt new planning angles for old properties. Just as in most commercial endeavours, innovation and imagination are rewarded. To rely upon your agent's findings and your architect's approach would mean little of your own creativity entering the frame. You must build your own empire.

7 Be Decisive

Those dealers who are shown the most opportunities by agents are those who can act quickly and firmly. A property sale is a process which can drag on endlessly and then collapse just prior to consummation. There are brigades of time-wasters who will assure all concerned that they want to buy – and then they'll pull out at the last minute through a fit of nerves. Make sure you are not among this insufferable breed, because if you are you will never establish a decent reputation in the agents' fraternity. Moreover, word may spread that you are of no consequence, and that you break promises. You may then find that even agents with whom you've never dealt previously fail to take you seriously.

19

The agent's favourite developer is one who responds immediately to a proposition. The developer should organise to view and investigate the property as soon as he hears about it. He should keep appointments with agents. He should always tell an agent if such a deal is of no interest to save time – if that is the case. And the developer should only express firm interest if he means it. If you intend immediately turning a property, you should make the agent aware that this is a possibility. Always instruct the agent who found the property with the resales. And assuming the agent does a competent job, ensure you pay him his fee on full at the appropriate time. Foolish, small-minded developers try to knock agents on fees. This tactic rarely pays, since an agent can always sue and recover the money owed through the courts if need be. Even if the agent receives a sizeable sum for apparently doing nothing, he will be positive towards you next time – and if you make money, who cares if someone else does ok?

8   Understand Financing

These days complex financing arrangements mean half of property success lies in getting your money arrangements right. The range of residential mortgages available is now enormous, and can make a significant difference to the net cost of a home. In a similar fashion, there are many commercial property lenders, all offering different terms and demanding different conditions. You should be fully aware of all the relevant financing options, so as to pick the right source and type of borrowed money when doing a property deal. While in some cases a certain bank might appear to offer outstandingly cheap terms, it could pay to use the same institution as on a previous occasion, since the latter source will stick with you even if things go wrong.

Gaining an understanding of property finance does not mean you do away with the services of bankers, accountants, and mortgage brokers. It means that when you deal with these professional money-men, you know what to ask for and what ought to be possible. If you know where you can get money and how much it will cost – and whether a given deal will be acceptable to a lender – then you have a significant advantage over many in the property game.

9   Understand Property Law

Again, this does not mean you should sack your lawyer, draw up all your own leases and do your own conveyancing (although some of this is advisable on occasion). Rather it means you must know enough property law to realise what is possible – when for instance 'established use' may be a method of obtaining planning consent, or where enfranchisement of a house might be worthwhile. The law is the single most important discipline in relation to property transactions – one reason why many lawyers are so successful as property developers. The final details and tough legal decisions need to be referred to a sound solicitor, but you should have the groundwork so that he can talk sense to you about lease defects or a dubious title. With this knowledge you can save time and money when you talk with your lawyer, and be aware of more money-making opportunities.

The best way to acquire this expertise is not by becoming an article clerk to a City law partnership, but simply by getting involved in property transactions and showing willingness to learn. The vagaries of British property law will be revealed to you in the cut and thrust of deal-making, and before long you will have developed a solid understanding of the crucial facts, to which you can add as you buy and sell more.

10   Time Your Deals Right

This means you should time things carefully with regard to both your own financial position and the state of the property market. In the early days you should undertake one deal at a time and never stack up too much borrowed money at once. Not only will many deals need too much supervision, the possibility of two simultaneous crises – which might prove crippling – cannot be ruled out. Time your sales to suit, and as far as possible buy when you are flush, rather than strapped for funds. Always be aware of how fast property prices are moving, and which areas are accelerating in value fastest. Never move into a region if it has already topped out. Concentrate on a profitable property sector while it works, but do not be afraid to move into new waters if the deals disappear or competition becomes too intense. Most businessmen say being successful is a matter of being in the right place at the right time – property is no exception.

1

Become an Estate Agent

From John Ritblat to Harry Hyams, many of today's most successful property tycoon started their careers as estate agents. It is the perfect method to learn the rules of the property game and meet the big movers and shakers. And for many it is a marvellous way to scout around for deals. Although many within the trade call it a profession, there are no legal barriers to stop anyone acting as an estate agent. While a high proportion of agents are chartered surveyors, or have auctioneering or other qualifications, none of the official bodies has any statutory rights over the business of estate agency. This differs from the law, where the Law Society controls all solicitors, or for accountancy profession, where all members have to be chartered or certified so as to be allowed to audit. There are thus opportunities for any enterprising individual to start up a practice and possibly make a fortune.

Having suggested that estate agency is the ideal route to property dealing, few who trade for that purpose alone make it work. The agency must justify itself on normal commissions from sales of residential or commercial property. This means selling ability is required, since the field is now overrun by major groupings like Lloyds Bank and Prudential Assurance and various building societies. Many of these institutions can justify lower profits per branch than you can survive on, since they have economies of scale and can sell other products such as their own insurance and mortgages through the agency. While many have become fabulously wealthy in estate agency in recent years, it has generally been by selling out their business for huge sums, rather than transacting dozens of sales a week.

You will realise that the competition in virtually any area is now intense. The number of shop-fronts in London alone has soared in the last ten years from perhaps 2,000 to 4,000, while the number of homes in the city has increased only slightly, and the frequency with which people move only advanced from an average of every 5 years rather than every 7. So the vast majority of London agencies might only finalise two or three sales a week.

But one of the main attractions of the business is the relatively modest capital costs to start. One key ingredient is a decent shop unit. Interestingly, estate agents are classified as office-users, so a vacant shop will have to gain a change of planning consent before it can be used. A premium for a reasonable lease of anywhere between £5,000 and £50,000 might be payable, depending on the location, and rent could be anything up to £20,000 if it were a big shop in a busy high street. A decent standard of shop fitting is these days expected, which will cost around £8,000 or more. Working capital to pay staff and advertising costs could be another £15,000. It will take some months for any new agency to generate some instructions and a few months after that to sell and complete property sales and receive the commission. A useful way to help get started is to try to solicit half-commission work from rival agents. Jointly instructed agents can expect to earn around 2% on any sales (plus VAT) while sole agency is around 1%.

Good negotiators to work in your agency will not be easy to find. They might well expect a salary (including likely commission) of around £20,000, and a reasonable car – which is anyway necessary for their work. Traditionally estate agents have supplemented their bread and butter business by undertaking structural surveys for housebuyers and building societies – but you require a formal RICS or ASVA qualification to carry out such jobs.

24

Letting of residential property can be highly lucrative. Management of property brings in useful steady income for little effort. And many smaller agencies in less busy districts will carry out commercial sales and lettings and business transfers. The requirement for a proper training and experience of such matters as rate assessments and rent reviews mean small new outfits without qualified partners can find the going tough. Until recently no member of the major surveying organisation was allowed to be a Director and shareholder in an agency incorporated as a limited company. They were permitted to be associates. Nowadays a partnership structure is not required.

Most features of the trade are common sense. You need applicants to buy property and instructions to sell to them. You maximise exposure through press advertising, mail shots and mailbox drops, together with as many For Sale (together with a few bogus Sold) boards as possible. One law you should be aware of when entering this game is the Estate Agents Act 1979, which covers such areas as handling clients' money, and disclosure of a personal interest in any transactions. If you use the agency merely as a shop window to operate a dealing business (as do many so-called agents), then be careful. Every vendor who instructs you, and every applicant who is interested in your properties for sale, must be told of your interest – otherwise you face criminal prosecution.

If you do decide to set up your own firm, you ought to acquire some inner knowledge of the workings of an active agency. The better firms are always advertising for negotiators in local papers, the Estates Times or Estates Gazette. Try being a negotiator for three months and decide whether you can cope with rude clients and fierce competition, as well as the frustration of seeing deals fall through and rivals sell properties before you. If you take the plunge afterwards, set up shop in opposition to an old-fashioned style firm in an up-and-coming area with plenty of private housing changing hands – preferably a good deal of price inflation too.

As an estate agent you see the daily workings of the property trade and you meet all the important people. You may well make a tidy living just from the everyday instructions, and there is always scope for alighting across interesting opportunities for you as principal. But the hours are long – a seven day week is now common – and the competition never ending. But there can be no beating it for learning the ropes.

2

Letting Residential Property

Although over 60% of households own their homes, many still rely upon renting accommodation. With the supply of council rented property static in virtually all metropolitan areas, and demand from visitors and foreigners ever greater, there is a huge market for private landlord accommodation. But the field is littered with dangers, since the law is heavily biased against the property owner in favour of the tenant. Rafts of onerous legislation passed since the war mean landlords have to be flexible and cautious if they are not to end up with sitting tenants and a pathetic rental income.

Until the law changes, any new lettings should only be made as a holiday letting, a genuine company let, or under one of the exemptive cases referred to in the 1977 Rent Act, as amended. This is to enable the landlord to evict the tenant if necessary. A fair rent is a form of rent control supervised by rent officers employed by the local authority; any tenant, unless he rents under a special case, can apply to have his rent registered. This will nearly always be far lower than an open market rent – in many areas of London, registered rents are one tenth of the going market rate. All a tenant does is complete form RR1 available from the Citizens Advice Bureau. Any landlord who wishes to make money from letting residential accommodation would be well advised to ensure that the tenants do not register the rent.

Large properties in busy cities are one way to make money letting privately. Plenty of single prospective tenants need short-term rental accommodation, for which they may well be willing to pay a high rent. Each 'bedroom' can be let separately, in an attempt not to create a joint tenancy, and charge a higher pro-rata rent per room. This still technically creates a protected tenancy of the room itself, but sitting tenants in such a situation are unlikely. Alternatively the entire house can be let to say students. Generally it is more practical to charge an overall figure per month which includes all services and rates but excludes say telephones. It normally makes sense to obtain a coin box from British Telecom. Always demand at least one month's deposit and the first month's rent in advance. Keep a rent book and give the tenants a receipt for their deposits. You will have to declare the income to the taxman – there is a special section in your tax return where UK property rental income should be stated. You can deduct from it the costs of the letting, rates, and wear and tear.

Letting under the Rent Act should fall under either the Protected Shorthold Tenancy provisions, or Holiday Lettings. Shorthold tenancies cannot be for less than one year nor more than five, and are for agreed periods, during which the landlord cannot evict the tenant. But the landlord has the right to recovery of the property at the end of the tenancy. A property let strictly for holiday purposes is not protected by the Rent Act. And after any holiday letting the landlord can let the property for up to nine months for non holiday purposes and recover the property at the end of the term, as long as he officially states this to the tenants. Other exemptions include letting by an owner-occupier who is temporarily absent, and letting by servicemen. Fair rents can be agreed in these cases, but not with holiday lets.

Many people wishing to let property use specialist agents. These agents will charge around 10–15% of the gross rent payable as their fee to find tenants, collect rent, and administer the property. This cost can be offset against rental income for tax purposes. It depends how energetic you are as to whether you use them. Given the insatiable demand for good rental accommodation in most urban areas (especially South-East England), through inexpensive local classified advertising you can generally find tenants – so an agent will not be the only party able to let your property. And again, you should be able to structure a letting agreement using sample forms published by Oyez – perhaps with your lawyer's help – just as efficiently as any agent. When drawing up a tenancy agreement, include a full inventory of all furniture, and a schedule of the interior condition of the property. Agents may well have greater experience at choosing tenants than you. Many landlords prefer foreign nationals as tenants, since they feel they're less likely to want to stay and become sitting tenants.

Generally it is wise to find tenants with sound work and previous landlord references and respectable backgrounds. They are far more likely to want to move on or whatever in time to own their own property. Most agents try to coerce tenants into organising company lets – so that some corporate body stands behind the tenancy in the event of a default on the rent or damage to the property. Other devices used to get around the Rent Act are licences. Both these forms of letting are no protection if you have an awkward tenant who is willing to go to court, as a test case proved in 1985. Tenants paying full market rents can suddenly become sitting tenants paying minimal rents, and the capital value of the property can be reduced by as much as 50%.

If the landlord resides in the building, then the tenants are treated as lodgers and have no tenancy rights. The more services – such as breakfast – that a landlord provides for the tenants – the better confirmation that no letting with Rent Act protection has been created. Obtaining mortages from conventional sources such as building societies for properties which you wish to let out can be difficult. The less well-known banks and building societies and insurance companies are the most "available" sources for this type of purchase. Lenders are quite rightly wary of using as security a property which may end up with sitting tenants, whom they cannot evict, even if they re-possess the property if the owner defaults on the mortgage. They will sue the owner and be obliged to sell the property at auction for perhaps 60% of its vacant open-market value.

The overall message to prospective landlords is that to let your property without adequate preparation and hope that your tenants do not take advantage of their tenancy rights is a dangerous game. The courts take a dim view of landlords taking the law into their own hands and trying to "winkle" tenants by bursting boilers and loosening slates. Such behaviour is of course a criminal offence. It is nowadays all too easy for tenants to become fully aware of the opportunities to register rents and become a permanent fixture. Many young couples have obtained their initial deposit on a house of their own by forcing a landlord to pay a hefty cash sum to them to persuade them to vacate. You do not want to end up paying out sums like this. Plan ahead and make sure any tenancies are unprotected. In this way it is possible to generate excellent income streams and benefit from the capital appreciation of the residential property. The surplus income can be used to pay off interest on loans taken out to buy further rental properties. In this way one can build up a portfolio over the years of income generating residential properties. If you are a reasonable and careful landlord, you are actually doing a service to the community, through the provision of accommodation to those who would otherwise find it difficult to move to that area.

3

Buy at Auction

Auctions are wholesale property markets, and generally attended by dealers rather than individual buyers. Most properties put up for sale at residential auction are properties with problems or potential. Either the property is in need of renovation or more could be made of it through development. Auctions are also a popular venue to sell such items as building land, freehold ground rents, and residential tenanted property. And of course auctions cope with considerable quantities of commercial property such as offices, light industrial and shops. This section will focus primarily on residential property auctions, since these are more accessible to novices.

The key point to note about auctions is that any sale is instant, final and binding. After the auctioneer's gavel (hammer) has gone down, the property is sold absolutely. Even if you are acting as agent, you will be treated as principal buyer if you bid. English property law allows considerable dithering and time-wasting when sales are conducted by private treaty; there can be no such luxuries with auctions. You should therefore be in a position to judge carefully whether a given property is worth the amount being asked for, since if you bid, you could end up owning the thing – with no escape routes! If you do buy and fail to complete, you can be sued for any shortfall if the property is re-sold, and you will lose you deposit, and will have to pay the vendor's costs. Normally you will be required to pay 10% in the auction room on the spot, and the balance within 28 days. Consequently to buy at auction you either have to possess the liquid resources, or have definite bank or mortgage finance available. Overall, auctions are not for amateurs, but for brave people who do their homework and know their limit.

The major London auction houses such as Willmotts, Barnard Marcus and Hillyers publish monthly catalogues free to callers. These contain perhaps 250 lots ranging in value from £5,000 to £500,000. Guide prices – which are not reserves, but higher – are now given in some catalogues, and can be quoted over the phone. Keys are often available to view these lots, and every opportunity should be taken to carefully inspect any building you are especially interested in, judging by the catalogue description and picture. Other lots are open on special arranged viewings. These occasions should be exploited to the maximum in order at the least to learn about property in general. The area and structure of the building should be studied, and the possibilities for improvements, extensions or conversions considered. Unless you become especially interested in a specific lot, it is not worth hiring a qualified structural surveyor to accompany you on auction lot viewings to carry out full surveys. His charges will rapidly mount up, while you may find yourself being outbid in the room every time – even if you liked the property. If you become particularly concerned about major structural defects, it is best to steer clear and aim for a safer property, since there is no comeback if you buy it.

The unpredictability of auctions creates opportunities and dangers. There are occasions when lots get knocked down very cheaply simply because no-one standing in the room happens to be interested. There are also times when bidders get wildly carried away bidding against each other, and end up paying far more than they wanted to – and more than the property is worth. It must be stressed that most residential lots are being auctioned for a reason. This may not be apparent from a cursory viewing of the property. Quite often leasehold premises offered in auction have onerous covenants or restrictions, or only a short term left unexpired. In other cases there may be dubious planning consents or cautions on the title. In other cases, vendors will sell by auction simply to demonstrate a full open-market price has been achieved – out of probate, for instance. In other cases, the vendor is desirous to achieve a quick sale – such as building societies with foreclosed houses. Other frequent users of auctions are local authorities, the government, and the various nationalised industries such as British Rail. It is essential to vet the "special conditions of sale" supplement which accompanies a catalogue. Local searches might well uncover such nasty items as a Closing Order or a Listed Building Order. If need be legal advice should taken – although again, if you ask a lawyer to undertake much work on auction possibles, you may spend a great deal for no return.

Arranging finance to buy auction lots is not a simple matter. Most banks will only agree in principle to support a purchase but require details of the specific property against which they would take security. You could be in the position of buying a lot and finding the bank will not come up with the 70% or 80% they promised in theory, if they don't like the property. The best situation to be in is being able to secure borrowings against other assets, or best of all having the liquid cash available yourself. There are various rather expensive finance houses who insist they specialise in auction property finance, but in reality they simply offer the same type of deal as your High Street clearing bank – but quite possibly at stiffer rates of interest.

There are quite a number of full-time property dealers who make a prosperous living by dealing in properties at auction. They have an eye for a cheap lot, and snap it up intending to turn it to a builder or owner-occupier. They rarely invest for the long term, but make a margin (or sometimes lose money) by selling on. They are willing to buy "blind", having not viewing the property or studied the conditions. You should not try to emulate them. They have a highly developed feel for property value and a superb network of contacts to sell on to. And they have the money to tide them over bad deals!

There are certain games played in the auction room which potential auction dealers should know about. One is when a possible bidder stands up and points out say a serious notice served on the property which is not in the particulars. This is often a ploy to put others off, and clearly demonstrates the interest of the party concerned. If you have canvassed the property you should have come across the problem anyway. Another device, this time used by the auctioneer, is to take bids "off the wall". These are invented bids which give an impression of interest in the lot when there is none. In other cases the vendor will buy his own lot in if the auction fails to reach the reserve and potentially places an embarrassingly low valuation on the property. Another, more sinister practice occasionally found in auctions is where a "ring" of connected dealers knowingly bid against each other and attempt to keep others out. Once the lot is knocked down to them, a second auction then takes place among the dealers, one of whom consequently secures the property more cheaply.

If you become extremely interested in a specific lot, it is always possible to put in an offer to the auctioneer's office ahead of the auction day. Some vendors will sell prior if not much interest has been shown and you make a seemingly decent price. Auctioneers tend to advise clients not to accept offers ahead of the auction, since it generates less excitement for the attendees on auction day. Perhaps more lucrative is examining what is not sold in auction and attempting to buy it afterwards. A post-auction list is published a few days following the event which reveals the reserves placed on the unsold lots. Normally an offer marginally above the reserve – and sometimes well below it – can secure the lot. But since speed will be of the essence to vendors, an immediate exchange of contracts will still be expected.

If you wish for whatever reason to sell by auction,

apply either to a local auctioneer or to one of the very big outfits like Allsops (for commercial property). Usually you will have to book a lot two months ahead of the auction date. The fixed cost is around £200, and the usual 2% fee will be charged if the lot is sold at any time from instruction until a month after the auction. You should fix a reserve and discuss it with the auctioneers, and supply keys for vacant properties.

The Estates Gazette publishes an excellent weekly section detailing recent auctions, and carries all the major auction houses' adverts giving dates and locations. There are probably 10 or so worthwhile auctions a month in London, lasting anything up to three days.

4

Raise Bank Finance

Building society mortgages are the natural first method to pay for one's abode. They offer competitive rates of interest, they are generally for 25 years, and they are reasonably straight-forward to obtain. But very few organisations are willing to extend mortgages for the purchase of second and subsequent properties. The building societies (and other competitor lending organisations) burnt their fingers during the 1974 property crash with speculative loans to property developers, and now tend to have strict rules against lending for such purposes. So if you want to buy either residential or commercial properties which you are not to live in – where do you go?

The obvious answer is your local clearing bank. Banks have always been the first source of finance for property dealing and investment, and the four major high street banks are all active in this area. Finding the support of a good branch manager can be a major stepping stone to property success. As a first port of call try your own branch. Initially approach the manager and tell him of your plans without taking a specific proposal. He will probably outline whether in principle he would be willing to lend you money for a development and how much and at roughly what rate. A reasonable bank should talk around 3% over base. You can also expect a 1% arrangement fee for a facility. Normally you should request an overdraft rather than a fixed term loan, since you can then draw the money down as needed, without having expensive borrowed money sitting idle in your account before it is required.

Giving a persuasive and slick bank presentation is an

important ingredient for success when asking for money. Include in the presentation quotes from builders, and details of the builder who will actually carry out the work, a photograph of the property, estimated resales from local agents with supporting evidence, and a cash flow forecast of the job. Show the manager that you have considered everything, since he needs to feel confident in your abilities. You should therefore not promise what you are unable to deliver; if you let your bank down, it will not forgotten. At each stage in a project keep your bank manager in touch – especially keep him informed of problems – they will normally be sympathetic and helpful. But if you spring terrible news at a late stage, he will be much less happy, and may take evasive action, such as calling in an overdraft or serving a winding up notice.

The bank will want a first charge on the property as first lenders. Before they agree any deal, they will want a valuation from you, and will also send out a local manager just to give the property a glance over. You will I'm afraid have to pay for this. They will generally give some percentage of the forced sale value of the property. Typically you will be able to borrow 70% of the valuation. As you renovate the property, you can argue that its value is increasing, so therefore you should be able to borrow more. In this way you may be able to obtain further finance to help pay for some of the building works. In these instances the bank might require a Clerk of Works completion certificate at each progressive stage of the renovation. But clearly banks will never lend 100% of the money needed to do a deal – you have to find other finance. In speculative development projects banks are concerned to have security for their money, and so three-quarters of the value of the project at any stage is generally as much as they'll lend.

Avoid giving a personal guarantee as well as security on the major property. All decent lenders nowadays offer non-recourse lending save the security of the mortgaged building. Bankers are loathe to lend without security for any purpose, but when they lend for property development – which will always offer excellent security – they argue that it is "speculative" and should therefore be at a higher rate of interest! They win all ways. You can of course attempt to borrow more than 70% by offering further property or shares or gilts etc. as security. The danger with this is that if virtually all the money is borrowed, the interest repayments are going to be painfully high. You should of course always allow for the cost of borrowing on all borrowed money for the duration of the project until sale monies are received. A typical calculation of a project financing might be useful at this stage.

Cost of house:	£75,000
Legal fees, stamp etc.	£1,000
Conversion into 2 flats:	£10,000
Selling costs, legal etc	£2,000

If all the money is borrowed, and the project takes 5 months from payment to receipt of sale monies, then interest will be approx $5/12 \times 13\% \times £81,000$ (average amount of capital) = £4,387.

Hence total costs = £76,000 + £12,000 + £4,387 = £92,387

If the flats sell for £55,000 each, the total proceeds on sale will be £110,000, leaving a net pretax profit of around £17,600 – a good return for five months' work.

Clearly it is important in your early deals to demonstrate reliability to your bank manager.

Bank finance costs more than building society borrowings. So why use it? Firstly, overdrafts are totally flexible, in that you can draw down the exact amount you need each day – and only that amount – and you will only pay interest on such borrowings. Secondly, banks will not be so shirty about the condition of the property. Many building societies will entirely turn down dilapidated houses, since they worry that it might prove difficult to sell. Thirdly, banks are generally much faster than building societies. While any conventional mortgage and life cover takes at least three weeks (and often, for unpredictable reasons, longer) to obtain, once you've got a secured bank facility, the overdraft draw-down can be organised in days. Hence it is well nigh impossible to use building societies to borrow money for auction properties. Moreover, most building societies do not allow you to rent out the property, and are not interested in mixed commercial/residential properties such as freehold shops and upper parts. And the residential lease in normally expected to be at least 20 years longer than the term of the mortgage – meaning a minimum lease length of 45 years. As a sting in the tail, plenty of building societies will charge a penalty of three months' contributions if you try to rapidly turn around and sell the flat/house within a year. Look out for this clause when buying a home using a standard mortgage – you never know how quickly you might want to move.

An understanding bank manager has been quoted by many successful men and women as a major benefit on their way to riches. If you can gain the trust of a manager, he will be willing to listen to proposals and extend help when he can. Few have made big bundles without borrowing money, and after all the banks do profit from it – as long as you repay them! Make sure you keep the manager informed, even if problems occur, and he will like you the more for it. There is little to choose between the four major clearing banks – what matters is finding a manager willing to back you. I hope you find one.

5

Do Your Own Surveys

Most buyers of residential properties have them structurally surveyed beforehand by a professional chartered surveyor. He will attempt to decide whether the property is in a sound condition, and if there are defects, how extensive they are and what they would cost to repair. Commissioning a survey of this sort is voluntary, unlike the conventional building society/bank "valuation survey", which is normally much briefer and essentially undertaken on behalf of the lender (although you pay for it!). Structural surveys will normally carry some sort of guarantee, so that if quite obvious and serious faults quickly emerge, legal action may be taken against the surveyor who should by rights have spotted them. But generally a survey will be written in such a fashion that makes it difficult to sue the author.

Savings

The difficulty with structural surveys is that they are expensive and frequently not greatly illuminating. A typical three-bedroom house in London may well cost £300 for a proper survey, which might take over a week to prepare. If you are looking at a number of properties with a view to buying just one, you could easily end up spending over £1,000 just on survey fees. The British property-buying legal system means one tends to chase numerous properties to buy which fall through before the deal is done. But prior to the deal breaking down it may have been necessary to have a good idea of the structural condition and the cost of works needed. All this points to the sense of learning the rudiments of doing a survey oneself, so one can judge whether to proceed with a deal.

Equipment

Professional surveyors come equipped with various pieces of expensive tools such as Protimeters to test damp. If you can borrow one of these, fine – if not you will be obliged to use common sense. They can also be hired from hire shops. One essential item is a good torch – there are always dark areas which need to be searched. Take a stout screwdriver to probe wood for rot, and perhaps a pair of binoculars to inspect roofs and chimneys. Most important of all, take a clipboard, note-pad and pen, to record site notes.

Roofs

While most houses now are built with tiles, many existing properties still have slate roofs, which tend to be weaker and more prone to damp penetration since they will be older. But slates should last for 100 years, whereas tiles are normally only good for 60. Look for rusted nails which lead to missing slates. Look through the attic – you should not be able to see the sky. Check carefully the lead flashing which should be water-tight. Newer roofs will use zinc rather than lead, which is more expensive. On flat asphalt roofs, look for cracks and signs of age; these type of coverings have a limited lifespan. Lead flats have longer lives, but tend to expand and contract with temperature, and so should have joins which can cope with this movement. Anywhere where water accumulates tends to produce a leak. Chippings on bitumen felt roofs often cover defects below – be suspicious. Check guttering and rainwater pipes to see they are secure and do not permit the escape of water at joints. A thorough internal inspection of the underside of the roof should be carried out to look for timber infestation. A fine dust pinpoints furniture beetles. If there is serious infection, specialists must come and spray the property, and quite possibly the offending timbers should be cut out. Check chimney stacks for sulphate attack, which weakens the brickwork and leads to decomposed mortar.

Walls

Rendered walls and simple brickwork present fairly straight-forward faults if they occur. Serious leaning suggests considerable subsidence and major expense. Cracked rendering can lead to serious underlying damp and indicates settlement, while mortar reduced to dust severely weakens brickwork and should be replaced. Internal rising damp in the skirting indicates a defective dpc and specialists will be required to provide an injected replacement. Some older properties have no damp proof course, and since most building society lenders insist upon one, a specialist damp installing company will have to be contracted. Fractures in the brickwork between two structures indicates settlement in the foundations, possibly caused by thermal movement or water movement in the soil. Problems with the foundations normally require underpinning, which is the disruptive pumping of concrete into the ground after excavation. A crack in a ground floor window from the sill to the ground suggests foundation heave in clay subsoil.

Floors and Staircases

These items are probably more prone to defects than any other, thanks to dry rot, wet rot, and pipe intrusion. Examining floors in occupied houses is difficult, since carpets etc. cannot be removed to gain access. Look in areas such as under lavatory basins and sinks and behind baths and wcs. Expect relatively uneven floors in old properties, but be highly suspicious in new properties with askew floors.

Dry rot is caused by poor ventilation of underfloor timbers and rising damp. Look for small, brown discolouration, cracking of timber and fruiting bodies (fungus). Rising damp will leave a white stain. Well constructed staircases should not creak or vibrate underfoot. Check the stair balustrades – they are expensive to replace.

Drainage

Serious surveyors carry out tests to ensure the drain system is watertight, using smoke or pneumatic or hydraulic techniques. These are complex and time consuming, and would not normally be attempted by an amateur, but a detailed visual inspection is well worthwhile to try to determine any visible damp patches adjacent to drains or guttering.

Internal Finishes

Inspect wall and ceilings for plaster cracks – severe shrinkage may necessitate replacement of the entire surface. Check wood panelling for rot infestation. Look at skirting boards and door frames for pinholes and sawdust – this indicates beetle infestation. Check plaster walls with a moisture meter. Shrivelled timber skirtings indicates dry rot, while cracks running along the grain of external frames suggests wet rot. There are in addition a host of painting defects, which are all too apparent to the eye. These range from flaking to crazing to chalking to blistering, and usually indicate poor workmanship or age.

Services

This includes water supply, electricity supply, gas supply, and heating supply. Excessive numbers of cold water joints means the pipework is vulnerable to frost. If water from the taps is sluggish then pipe sizes are inadequate. A sluggish hot water discharge with encrustation around the tap outlets indicates furred pipes. Try to discover if any servicing has been carried out on the boiler. Checking electrical systems is the work of a specialist; if you have doubts, you must contact one to do the work for you.

Although the foregoing is a very brief summary of some items to look out for, it covers many of the essential points. The most important thing to do when undertaking a survey is to take one's time and cover the entire property. Then common sense will normally alert one to major defects, even if minor problems are missed. If you have carried out your own amateur survey and you've identified problems – but still wish to proceed with the purchase – you might then be advised to employ an expert, in order to accurately assess the extent of the problem. This also produces an authoritative and unbiased report, with which you can beat down the asking price.

6

Getting Planning Permission

Obtaining favourable planning consent is a dramatic way
of enhancing the value of a property. Certain professional dealers specialise in undertaking this alone – simply
buying plots or houses and gaining worthwhile consents
and then selling the property on without having done
any work. Getting planning permission is essentially a
cheap process. Architects' fees are low on the promise of
the job of the ultimate development, there are minimal
lawyers' fees, and none of the perils of construction and
builders. But gaining permission for a change of use or
significant works is rarely easy, since development of
surburban areas has increased the urge to preserve
among local authorities.

The law regarding planning permission is fairly technical, and if you wish to tackle planning situations with
serious intent, you should enlist the support of an able
lawyer. Indeed, a capable property solicitor is almost a
prerequisite for success in the field. Without his intimate
knowledge and experience of the various wrinkles to
look out for in leases and site plans, you will make many
blunders. And remember, each mistake when dealing in
the property world is likely to be in the thousands of
pounds level. Lawyers may charge by the hour – a good
firm of solicitors will link a fee to the success of the deal
and extract a fee of perhaps a percentage of the value of
the transaction. In addition to a lawyer you may well
require an architect to draw up plans when applying for
planning permission. Try to obtain a personal recom-
mendation, and always ensure you have an idea before
any work is undertaken of the cost involved. There is also
a new breed of advisor called Planning Consultant. They

47

can be found in most Chartered Surveyors' practices. They are often ex-planning officers, and have an intimate knowledge of planning procedures, and the policies and personalities involved in any particular area. These specialists may be too expensive to use at the planning application stage but they are essential if you wish to proceed.

The classic planning permission which boosts the value of a property is a change of use of a large old house into two or more separate flats. You can get a reasonable idea of the local authority's attitude from the extent of similar properties which have been converted in the same way. The Local Borough Plan will designate the authority's attitude to such applications. Considerations such as the provision of street services like sewers, the availability of parking space, and the intensity of habitation will be important. Where a house has achieved an established use since 1964 as separate flats say, then you can apply for permission to formally convert. The process is however long-winded and tortuous. Frequently neighbours or other interested parties will put up objections which can block your attempt at the last hurdle. You should look at the planning records to see whether or not there is a precedent for your proposals in the same street.

When viewing properties which seem suitable for conversion, take a cynical attitude towards vendors or agents who assure you that consent "will be no problem". Any serious vendor will have himself applied for and obtained whatever consents he can. Using options can save huge amounts of money and time for amateur landowners when applications are made. You should be aware that the present government has a policy not to refuse planning permission for residential development except where there is a positive alternative use. Consequently a lot of Labour local authorities are having their policies kicked out when applicants appeal against a planning refusal. So in many cases it can be worth considering.

7

Collect Ground Rents

Ground rents are freeholds (or less often leaseholds) of properties sold off on long leases. Generally a pepper-corn annual rent is payable. A typical freehold ground rent might be three annual payments of say £50 secured upon three self-contained flats, all part of a single house conversion. Each flat would have been leased for either 99 or 125 years from the date of first sale after conversion. Ground rents might be as high as £150 per residential unit in smarter addresses; frequently they will rise by one third of the original sum every 33 years.

Accompanying the ground rents will go various re-sponsibilities of upkeep as the landlord of the entire premises. The original purpose of granting leases and not flying freeholds for flats was in order to ensure that the cost of major but unevenly divided works, such as repairs to the roof or foundations, were distributed fairly across the leaseholders. In groups of apartments such as man-sion blocks, there will be common parts and frequently common services such as heating and a caretaker. The landlord is obliged to provide these and spread the cost amongst the flat-owners.

Negligent landlords do not bother and consequently the overall premises fall into disrepair. This can be wit-nessed in some fine locations such as St John's Wood. Often many of the flats are still occupied by sitting tenants paying paltry registered rents which don't even cover the rates. So the landlord chooses to forget his obligations and allows the block to rot. In others, dis-putes flare up because the landlord uses expensive agents to manage the premises for perhaps a 15% fee, and old-fashioned heat and refuse systems cost more than they should. The landlord is technically not allowed to make a profit out of orgnising the common services. But unscrupulous individuals will slip in inflated costs into the service charge and hope to take a cut themselves. The leaseholders will have difficulty proving the fraud and the law regarding duties and privileges of landlords in such circumstances is weak.

Leaving aside such nefarious methods of turning a surreptitious profit, ground rents can generally be judged as a pure income stream for a capital outlay. Normally residential ground rents which have no special features and plenty of time to run are valued at between 6 and 10 years' earnings – they consequently offer a gross yield of between 10% and 16% on the original investment. This rental income is treated in a similar way to earned income, and assuming you are a higher rate tax payer will be subject to 40% tax. Thus a freehold house with three flats sold on 99 year leases each with an annual ground rent of £50 might sell for $7 \times 3 \times 50 = £1,050$. For a 40% taxpayer this gives an initial net yield of 8.6%, which is competitive with bank interest rates – at present.

Of course there are much less simple ground rent freeholds. Many freeholds where 99 and 125 year leases were sold some time ago now have leaseholds which are quite short – that is, reversionary. There is thus potential to sell lease extensions to the existing leaseholders, in order that they make their leasehold interest more attractive to buyers. If the leaseholder allows his lease to expire he becomes a sitting tenant and will pay a registered rent, but no longer has any leasehold interest in the property. So if he then moves or dies or can be legally evicted, the vacant flat reverts to you, the landlord. In the case of leasehold houses the leaseholders may have the right to enfranchise and oblige the landlord to sell the freehold. But again, large capital sums may be payable.

Once a flat lease is shorter than 25 years, unless it is situated in a special area (such as parts of the Cadogen estate in Chelsea), then building societies will refuse to grant a mortgage. Thus potential buyers will be unable to raise finance on the premises. It therefore pays the short-leaseholder to buy a lease extension. For a 50 year lease on a 2 bed flat worth say £90,000 (if it had a 99 year or longer lease) a tenant might expect to pay £5,000 for the necessary 49 year extension. If you have liquid funds, there are opportunities to buy shorter leasehold flats quite cheaply from distressed leaseholders and then bargain for an extension offering cash to the freeholder. The extended lease can then often be worth more than the cost of original lease and the extension – but tying up such deals can be tricky. The landlord will try to tally all the extensions. An alternative might be to sell on the entire freehold to the tenant – but for much more than a simple 7 times ground rent.

Ordinary ground rents can be considered comparable to fixed-interest securities like gilts. Many buyers collect them as mini pensions, offering a sound yield for years to come. While the income is secure, the capital worth of the ground rent freehold is likely to vary with interest rates – worth a lower multiple as interest rates rise. In this respect they are similar to government bonds with a fixed coupon. It is worth bearing in mind the illiquidity of such investments – generally they are sold at auction – and the costs of dealing in them – agent and legal fees and stamp duty. Occasionally a freehold with ground rents may contain some hidden asset development, such as a roof-space which can be built upon or vacant land which may be redeveloped. In these cases the capitalised ground rent income and the redevelopment potential of the site will be married to obtain a total value. Commercial ground rents are also available, although much less frequently. Normally the rent payable is geared to the rack rent of the premises erected on the site. This means the ground rent is reviewed at the same time as the rack rent and rising proportionally. Such investments are similar to ordinary commercial purchases in terms of growth, but offer better security. Consequently the years' purchase required to obtain one is likely to be higher than for the rack rent – i.e., the yield is lower.

The major owners of commercial and residential ground rents are insurance companies and pension funds, and applying to them is one way of buying ground rents. These institutions are happy to own such secure, but long-term investments. Some property companies specialise in buying ground rents available on below-average multiples and turning them. Money can be made by buying ground rents and packaging them up to sell piece-meal to flat owners. Very often now flat leaseholders in a house will club together and buy the ground rent freehold using a jointly-owned shelf company. In this manner they can more comfortably control their own repairs and outgoings, rather than relying upon an uninterested landlord.

8

Find Shop Upper Parts

In major cities like London, many areas previously derelict have been gentrified in recent years. The incidence of home-ownership has created an insatiable demand for flats. Many secondary shop parades built between 1870 and 1940 have living accommodation above the retail area on the first and higher floors. While in the past building societies would be loathe to grant mortgages on long leases on such upper parts, nowadays the practice is much more acceptable. With a growing market for such units, a specialist group of developers have sprung up focusing on refurbishing and marketing these first-time buyer flats – and achieving excellent returns.

Shop freeholds are held by many different groups. Often if the parade is broken the retailer himself will own the property outright. In such circumstances, he would frequently live upstairs, and have a mortgage secured on the entire premises. In other cases big insurance companies, private property companies or public property companies might own the freeholds and collect a rent from the shop operators. The shopkeeper may simply have a lease on the shop outlet on the ground floor, but more frequently will lease the entire unit, since historically he and his family have lived upstairs. While this practice may be true among some ethnic groups, the rise of the multiple retailers and non-resident managers have seen a decline of owner-occupiers of this type.

So in many cases the flat or flats upstairs are vacant or sub-let. If left vacant, often for fear of sitting tenants, or for some minor storage use, there is potential to improve and sell off the premises on a long lease as a desirable abode. While the prices fetched for flats above shops do not compare with good purpose built units in a purely residential setting, in central city locations they can fetch excellent prices. The prices achieved can all too often be way in excess of the price the shopkeeper thought was possible – or indeed the landlord.

The tendency is for there to be a single unit above a shop, frequently a maisonette of two or three bedrooms on two or more floors. A crucial requirement is a separate entrance to the residential upstairs. Clearly no sale can be consummated if the buyer has to walk through the shop to get to his flat! How one goes about getting hold of these properties is pot luck. A starting point might be to locate a likely-looking secondary parade, in a central site but with upper parts seemingly unused. Wander into the shops and try to determine who owns the freeholds. Frequently local authorities do. Avoid retail outlets with such noxious trades as dry cleaners, chip shops and restaurants. Few people, however desperate they are to buy their own place, will want to live above the smell of curry every night. If you do buy a flat on a new lease, try to persuade the vendor to insert a clause in the lease restricting the use of the shop, so that such trades cannot start if the ownership of the downstairs unit changes (which is always possible!).

Doing building works above a busy shop can be problematical, especially if such major undertakings as a new roof are needed. Again, try to obtain the approval of the shopkeeper beforehand if he is the vendor. Explain that any upgrading of the overall accommodation should improve the outlook for his shop. There are of course dangers that you buy a leasehold flat against the wishes of a downstairs tenant, who then causes difficulties. It is always best to do a deal with the approval of the resident shopkeeper whe e possible, without scaring him into thinking that any improvements will be translated into a substantially higher rent upon the next review.

In some situations where there are three large floors of residential accommodation above a shop there can be potential for planning permission to convert the unit into several flats. In these situations one will almost always make more money converting into two or three than keeping as one. The market in maisonettes above shops can be sluggish, while studios and one bed flats will always sell quickly. Do not rely entirely upon a brief conversation with the planning officer on the phone. Take an architect's advice and draw up plans for outline permission. Check whether neighbouring shops have subdivided upper parts – look to see how many door buzzers there are. As an example:

Buy upper part for £40,000:
(a) Spend £10,000 making it into good 3B flat, sell for £75,000, making £15,000 pretax after all costs; or better still –
(b) Get planning permission for 2 1B flats. Spend £16,000 on works, sell each for £45,000 – total £90,000. Costs are around £70,000 in total, giving profits of £20,000.

This is an idealised example, but shows how splitting a unit will almost always pay – unless you are dealing with a detached residence in special circumstances.

Sometimes you will find shop upper parts with sitting tenants. These tenants might well be quite separate from the shopkeeper below, and may well be paying a tiny registered rent. Firstly determine whether they want to move. If they do not, try offering them cash or other inducements. Such bribery or winkling is common and legal. Tenant harassment is not legal – both civil and criminal actions can be brought against you. It is generally poor business practice, leaving aside the dubious morality, since if local authorities and estate agents hear of your antics, they will make life difficult and shun you respectively. Decide before you go ahead with any such deal whether you want to play the waiting game of having sitting tenants. Nowadays buyers will pay up to 60% of full vacant possession value for occupied property, hoping the tenants will suddenly move or expire.

But until any unit is vacated, the capital returns are poor – frequently a yield of a few percent. To play this game you need substantial resources. Generally beginners would be well advised to stick to vacant stuff and make quick, but perhaps lesser turns.

Shop upper parts offer an excellent area for a beginner since they tend to be quite cheap and broadly neglected by major property players. They are however a specialist niche and require a good lawyer experienced in dealing with such leases.

9

Design Beautiful Interiors
and Layouts

Many agents say that kitchens and bathrooms sell flats. To an extent they are right. Potential purchasers are highly influenced by the quality of the decorations and fittings in a home. It is possible to achieve much higher resale prices by producing impressive interior finishes. While the extra expenditure might be slight compared to the entire cost of the project, the added touches can up the price by 10% or more.

The more expensive locations and grander residences benefit most from the smart finishes. The best kitchen units and fitted bedrooms are now expected by top notch buyers, and you should be prepared to spend upwards of £15,000 on the kitchen and bathroom if the flat or house is in the classy area of town. In really splendid areas like Knightsbridge, it can even pay to fit a Jacuzzi in the bathroom and Poggenpohl in the kitchen. Better decorators and high quality wallpaper and paintwork will be necessary. Features such as video entry-phones and air conditioning are becoming more frequent – foreigners paticularly like them.

Catering for the upmarket buyer who wants a fine home doesn't just involve the finishes, however. The plan of the home should be designed with these fussy purchasers in mind. It can pay to lose a bedroom and have an ensuite bathroom for each of the remaining bedrooms. Occasionally a big house converted into several units can profitably be turned back into a palatial mansion – known in agentspeak as an "ambassadorial residence". You should study the posh agents' selling literature for the pricy new developments to see which features they are pushing – these will be the extras which can act as selling points. Remember that when a potential buyer views a flat or house, the newer and more luxurious it appears inside, the more he may forget the ugly neighbouring houses, lack of parking or inflated price.

The bigger developers may well make use of the services of an interior designer to ensure a tasteful mix of furniture, curtain, carpet and wallpaper styles and colours. While the big boys can afford the extravagance of this nebulous breed, more modest developers would be well advised to avoid their clutches. With a few rare exceptions, interior designers charge a massive fee and do a job anyone with a few connections and a decent sense of design could equal. Many interior designers use the argument that they can buy more cheaply than you since they order in bulk. This is not so – they just get spurious discounts on more expensive furniture which has been marked up accordingly.

Of course not only are superbly equipped and furnished flats receiving top selling prices – they also fetch the best rents. Letting to big companies or wealthy foreigners has become an amazingly lucrative pastime for many London landlords in recent years. Not only are corporate lettings less likely to degenerate into registered rents and sitting tenants, but they want the finest for their employees. American and Japanese banks will pay £1,000 a week for the right flat in Central London. The tenants will also tend to be tidier and better behaved than many, since they know another executive from their firm will be using the premises after they've gone. Excellent deposits can be achieved, the rent is paid on time, and utilities and services are settled without difficulty.

Letting and selling flats to the Arabs has proved a gold-mine for many property-owners in W1, W2 and SW7 and SW3, but their presence and surplus spending power has dwindled as the price of oil has slumped from

$30 to $18 a barrel. Yet other groups are taking their place. The sudden Asian and German wealth of recent times, partly thanks to the relative strength of the yen and Deutschmark, has encouraged tourists from those countries to rent the most lavish accommodation. And the desertion of so-called "funk money" from Hong Kong ahead of the Chinese takeover has meant many rich Hong Kong citizens renting in London. Generally top class letting agents will give advice as to what features are expected. Double glazing for security, warmth and quiet is a must. Americans insist on air-conditioning. Most rich foreigners worry obsessively about security, so electronic alarms and decent Banham locks on doors and windows are needed. Many Middle Easterners will not rent property unless there is a 24-hour doorman/caretaker on the premises.

Many older features in homes are now highly sought after. Ornate fireplaces and original architraving adds considerable value to a property – preserve them if you can, and beware builders who offer to cart them away – such fireplaces can have great resale value. Ensure there is as much cupboard space as possible. Built-in wardrobes in fitted bedrooms are de rigeur for smart homes. Electrical points should be numerous and convenient. Fancy extras such as wiring to allow video-viewing in every room from one recorder are a plus, as well as such gimmicks as cable tv – where it's available. Use the best cushion flooring in kitchens, since the additional expense is small but the impression great. Don't get involved in fitting power showers in bathrooms unless you want to go to considerable extra cost. If you are working on a classy joint, have fine but simply coloured curtains fitted. You may only get the cost back, but they give the place a superb feel when it's being shown to prospective purchasers. In general use plain but not dowdy coloured wallpaper and paint – white is usually best. Leave it to the owner-occupier to inject their character into the interior. Consider leaving such wood items as bannisters plainly

59

varnished, rather than painted. If a sound paraquet floor exists, restore it and leave it varnished.

By using your imagination and suiting your market, preparing suitable interiors can add many thousands to the eventual resale price of a home. The aim should be to make it look attractive and smart, but there ought (unless say letting to visitors) to be room for the buyer to make it theirs.

10

Make Finders' Fees

Many professional property developers make handsome profits effectively acting as agents. They simply charge a fee to other dealers and developers for finding a deal or putting the third party onto a property. Other individuals who have neither the capital nor the courage to develop themselves will earn a full-time living discovering cheap property or land plots and selling the information to a genuine buyer. These people may be attached to the investment or development department of a formal estate agency, but more often they act as freelance, roving "runners", with minimal overheads or rules.

The attributes which make a runner are a wide range of agent contacts, and a similar portfolio of developer/ buyers. They are masters of charm and have fine memories for agents' names and faces. They are quite willing to secure the services of an individual negotiator with cash payments to him rather than the firm. Their livelihood depends upon hearing about the juicy part-vacant houses or unmodernised mansions before the crowd, and rushing around their list of clients finding a buyer. If the deal stacks up the buyer will not mind forking out a fee, since the vendor is paying the retained agent's fee. The fee charged will vary, but for a highly profitable proposition might be as high as 5%; for a more mundane transaction 1% or 2% would be the norm. This would probably only be payable at the time of the onward sale of the completed development.

Most runners are ex-agents. They will understand the trade and the mentality of the agents they deal with, and will have met most of them while attached to a firm. In a similar fashion the developers they sell to will have been clients of theirs. They will have acquired an understanding of values and building costs and the intricacies of say assembling a site for development. While their success rate may be low and consummated deals infrequent, the fees on larger transactions can be superb – just imagine 3% of £600,000! (It's £18,000 for the lazy!) Anyone taking up this calling should be prepared to trudge long and hard before earning much – bear in mind most deals take months between first sighting and handing over of the loot.

Able runners can expect to be entertained by developers, since they are a prime source of deals. Quite possibly a runner can secure a salaried job with a major developer, and an added element of bonus depending on his hit rate. All the big housebuilders, for instance, will employ land-buyers – but they would normally be expected to have a surveying qualification or a degree in estate management. And this type of employment is not dramatically different to that of a negotiator at an estate agent. And most runners realise that they are likely to come across a whole range of deals, only some of which should be put to any one developer. One of a runner's skills is knowing a fellow who might specialise in say car park investments in a specific area, and another buyer of mansion block ground rents, and another dealer in terraced part-vacant houses with elderly tenants in a given district.

Since the runner is merely a broker who makes a commission, he avoids the developer's risk of acting as principal and the possibility of capital loss. However the competition in busy areas is tremendous. The runner has to be sure that he has at least a couple of sharp agents who will call him before anyone else, if he is to have a hope of success. As a runner is to all intents and purposes a second middle-man, there is also a grave danger of him getting squeezed out by mean developers. Thus the runner must "know his client" and be sure the developer will not renege on his obligations and realise the continuing value of keeping the runner happy.

A runner should be always alert to potential deals, even if they come from the most unlikely source. He should if necessary be prepared to pay a sub-fee to another information source, as long as a turn is made. Runners are always visible at the back of auction rooms making the acquaintance of all the key dealers, finding out who is really buying and who can be trusted. They should be determined individuals, who realise that no property deal happens of its own accord. They must undertake research with planners if necessary and ensure similar properties nearby are not cheaper. The luxury of being a runner is that just a few choice deals executed a year can mean four months annual holiday and a comfortable lifestyle. Yet a runner generally builds no great asset base, and relies upon his streetwise ability to discover cheap property for clients. Anyone looking at this field should enjoy the smell of the hunt, and be willing to put up with the infuriating antics of developers and agents. But a handsome lifestyle is maintained for a modest effort by most runners, who enjoy some risk without the fear of bankruptcy.

11

Buy via a Tender Offer

Tender offers lie somewhere between auctions and private treaty as a mechanism for selling property. They are a popular method among local or central government bodies for selling surplus land, and such diverse types as trustees for an estate and foreclosing building societies. They offer more secrecy and convenience of timing than do auctions. For complex properties with say considerable planning potential, they give possible buyers time to assess the proposition and concentrate on it.

Closed tender offers work by requiring all potential buyers to submit detailed and binding written offers by a fixed time and date. Your financing arrangements may have to be demonstrated. The agent acting for the seller will then open the various applications, and the highest bidder succeeds. Acceptance of your offer constitutes a binding contract, and you will be required to complete within 28 days. You must therefore have funds in place to execute the deal if you tender. Closed tenders give you time to plan exactly what you are willing to bid, and to inspect the quality of title and soundness of the building. You will be unable to determine what other bidders are offering, so you may end up pitching your tender way above theirs – and apparently paying too much. But if you can justify your price in terms of ultimate expected returns – it doesn't matter.

Open tenders are different in that acceptance of an offer does not in itself constitute a binding contract. Another phrase used is "informal tender". In these instances the seller will usually have a reserve but will want if at all possible to sell by the tender's closing date. So even if yours is the successful offer, the deal is not done, and will simply proceed along conventional private treaty lines. The beauty of auctions and closed tenders is that they are final – you cannot dither or hedge. You are forced to be decisive, one of the great traits of all master property dealers. Open or public tenders are available to anyone who applies for the tender documents. A private tender is conducted by putting the details of the offer to a select few developers who are the probable type of buyer. This system would only be used when the number of realistic bidders is under 15.

When making offers via tender, study the available documents hard. If the process involves putting forward plans which have to be approved by both planning authorities, the vendor – and perhaps even your financiers – do not go simply for the maximum square footage of highest value space. Bear in mind that Planning Committee council members are not interested in your profit – they care (supposedly) about the environment and the benefit – or disadvantage – the new structure will entail for the surrounding community. Mixed use schemes often win over purely commercial projects. The fairly mercenary insertion of such things as sheltered housing or housing association units may help your case. If the vendor itself is a form of public body, they will be concerned to see that they sell to an aesthetically sensitive builder, rather than a gumby who razes fine monuments.

Sharp dealers always hand in their tenders at the last minute. They are concerned that no-one is able to sneak a look at their offer and tell other friendly developers. This latter group could then submit slightly higher offers, using inside knowledge, and win. You would be advised to follow the same policy and have your offer biked round with just minutes to spare. It is amazing how sensitive information leaks when the sums involved are large.

Tenders generally apply to major schemes involving sums upwards of £250,000. It is an efficient method of selling plots of valuable development land and the like, but the costs involved in advertising and preparing for the sale mean it is usually not employed for straight-forward residential purchases. By all means try for properties or land so offered, but do not be too disappointed if your tender loses after much preparation beforehand.

12

Sell Well

There are a breed of developers who persistently appear to overpay for property, but still drive around in Rolls Royces and dine at the Ritz. They are masters of salesmanship, and know how to get the very best price for their developments. They use a variety of techniques to squeeze top prices, from wangling free plugs in the local press to instructing exactly the right agent to hiring a name interior decorator. But above all these skills they evolve a knowledge of the market they address, and a talent for persuading people to part with money.

In many situations there will be a "special purchaser". He is someone to whom a specific property is worth more than a market valuation would suggest. An example might be a leasee of a shop – he might be willing to pay more for the freehold of his shop than anyone else, simply because it gives him security and he becomes his own landlord. And again, a small "blackmail" strip of land between two large derelict buildings is worth far more to the owner of the two buildings than anyone else, since with it he can raze the entire site and develop it all afresh. And there are circumstances where a particular expansive retail chain will pay a huge premium for a shop lease where they are desperate for a unit in a given shopping centre.

The art lies in finding these special purchasers, or finding situations where the vendor of a property is not aware of a special purchaser who is known to you. Sometimes lots come up at auction which leaseholders would dearly like to buy but they fail to organise themselves properly in time. The astute dealer snaps up the lot and waits for the leaseholder committee to coordinate themselves and offer him a turn for his trouble. Another variation is the buying up of property due to be bought under a compulsory purchase order (CPO). Sometimes full values can be paid by councils and government and the compensation received remarkable.

When instructing agents, be selective about who you choose to market your property. Do not always listen to the agent who values your property higher than anyone else – he may just be bullshitting to get an instruction on his books. Have an appropriate agent work with you – use a snappy, modern firm to market brand new studio flats, and a more genteel outfit to handle a country cottage. It helps enormously if they have an office near the property – they will have more appropriate applicants and more passers-by interested in that area, and negotiators will be keener to whip people around the property at a moment's notice.

The ability to identify accurately real buyers and weed out time-wasters is a rare attribute. A fair number of people look round fine homes at weekends as a hobby, and have neither the willpower or the money to buy. Still other buyers will be negotiating over two other flats in addition to yours simultaneously. The fewer buyers you find who have to sell their homes, and may become involved in a chain, the better. Be suspicious of buyers who decide too quickly and offer too much and don't look to have the substance to complete – they are fantasists who clog up the system.

The flip side of finding special purchasers is to come across distress sellers. A typical example would be someone who has failed to meet their mortgage payments and is about to be foreclosed upon by the building society. They will always accept less than the market value for a quick deal, since if the building society forecloses, (a) they will never again be granted a mortgage; and (b) the building society will sell for even less and charge a lot for doing so – leaving the vendor with nothing, or even a bill at the end of it. Other examples of distress sellers might be shopkeepers willing to assign a lease for a nominal premium where they cannot afford to keep up payments, or divorcing or splitting couples who have bought a property in a joint name and now have to sell. Many follow the philosophy of buying when "Blood is running in the streets", as Baron de Rothschild said. If interest rates climb sharply, there will be many hurting speculators who can no longer afford to meet their financing commitments. The illiquidity of property means that they might well accept offers substantially below market for their properties, if it saves them from ruin. Certain over-extended plc property companies were in something of a pickle in October 1987 following the crash, but most have managed to sort their most pressing problems out.

Selling and buying are arts not sciences, and require natural gifts and experience. A thorough depth of knowledge of markets, prices, and buyers, and the financial condition of your seller (or potential buyer) always allows you to strike a better deal. An unemotional approach to the transaction helps too, since you then take note only of the facts – not hopes or desires. That is not to say you have to be cold to succeed in property – quite the reverse, you must be likeable. But when it comes to committing your money or accept cash from others, listen only to rational thoughts.

13

Dealing in Land

Britain is a crowded island with a constantly diminishing supply of land. The demand for housing or commercial land never ceases, and consequently any land with developmental potential is likely to increase in value. It is however worth noting that agricultural land has been a consistently poor investment during the 1980s, partly thanks to the slump in the UK farming industry. But virtually any urban land has its use, even abandoned quarries and swamps can be used as dumping grounds.

Land has certain obvious characteristics which are worth stating. Each parcel of land is immobile – each is unique – and each has an intrinsic locational value. Any piece of land has a highest best use in a given location – forestry might be suitable in the Scottish Highlands, while high grade offices more appropriate in EC3. Development profits are possible in built up areas where land is not exploited to its highest best use – a carpark in a city centre leased at a peppercorn ground rent, for instance, or old-fashioned residential gardens in sought-after sites at a resort location.

The frenzy of housebuilding activity by the major names such as Wimpey, Barratt and Beazer over recent years means spiralling prices are received for good housebuilding plots. Inflation in the price of such land in recent years in South-East England has beaten 30% per annum, and many such housebuilders have made a high proportion of their profits through gently selling their land banks. And around the periphery hundreds of up-and-coming housebuilders make perhaps 30 units a year.

It is not realistic to compete with the big boys for land

sales at auction or by tender or well-advertised private treaty. The classified columns of the Estates Gazette carry such offers, but they will be chased after by cash buyers who can pay more than you. The way to make a fortune in land is to identify plots without planning and buy them as vacant wasteland. Then get the relevant planning consents and sell on the enhanced plot. Look for areas of land immediately adjacent to existing buildings but with access and room to erect a fair sized house or two. Before preparing detailed drawings, take informal advice from an architect about the evenness of the land and attitude of local planners to new dwellings. Consider whether neighbours would object. An existing, but quite derelict structure would normally enable you to demolish it and establish a new home. Check with the planning authority that the site is zoned residential (or commercial, as the case may be). Send them tentative plans and try to obtain outline permission – the fee is around £50.

If outline consent is granted, certain matters will be reserved – siting, design and external appearance, means of access and landscaping. You will need to provide details of any trees to be lopped, alteration of access to the highway and parking spaces. The process is discussed in depth in the chapter on Planning, but in any event normally takes two to three months. Planners will be influenced by the intensity of dwellings and the quality of design. The more generous you are with space and the more in keeping the proposed buildings with existing structures, the higher your chances of success.

Country or town houses with massive gardens are a source of planning profits. By reducing the outsize garden and building a new residence on the leftover, one can buy a house and get the plot free. In the country land is worth perhaps 25% of the value of the property – in cities this rises to 40%. The figures can be much higher or lower percentages for commercial property, depending on the quality of building and location. Bigger plots introduce simple economies of scale, as the average cost of building a 3 bed house falls fast if you're building 25 at once rather than one on its own. If you buy very expensive land in sought-after locations, you must be sure to build the right sort of expensive property. Check into the adequacy of nearby services such as water drainage, sewerage, electricity, gas and telephone connections. Derelict land can also be a goldmine. Local authorities keep lists of these sites – some of which may have defects, such as contamination. Often however these plots are simply unused because they're too small for a large organisation like a local authority to use – but not perhaps too small for you to make money by developing. Another frequent situation is a passageway leading to a large open area at the rear of buildings – often used as an uneconomic builders' yard. Buying Ordnance Survey sheets enables you to identify such sites – along with a little touring by foot or bicycle (a car journey will not do – you travel too quickly!).

Land is often the subject of options or conditional contracts. If you spot a likely site and the vendor seems willing to sell, try to get him to grant you an option for say three months while you negotiate planning consent – or alternatively make the sale subject to this condition. These devices are most useful from your point of view: they limit your risk while committing the vendor to sell if you are satisfied the deal is right, and the down payment is not great. In the case of an option, he receives some monies outright, so even if no planning is granted and you do not exercise your option, he does not lose. A typical option sum might be 10% of the value of the site – if planning is received. You are free to exercise your option at any time up to three months after the initial granting of the option. If at the end of this time planning is still not achieved but there remains hope, an extension might be possible for a further non-returnable sum.

If you buy a plot of land and decide to sell, prepare your marketing campaign well in advance. Have a full plan drawn up with details of wayleaves and easements, and exact details of the tenure. If planning has been obtained provide both applications and consents. Even the making of a planning application can add value – even if only 'hope' value – it puts the property into play among developers. All too often auction property is sold "with planning applied for". Any relevant tenancies, agreements and licences should be included. You may choose to have a soil survey done to demonstrate there are no likely rock, subsidence or flooding problems. The major housebuilders will doubtless verify all your documentation using their own experts, but you demonstrate a professional attitude by providing such background material. It will also speed up any sale.

Probably the best way to sell residential land is by advertising in the Estates Gazette, since all the major buyers read the publication avidly. Alternatively you could instruct one of the London auction houses who are busy in this area, such as Jones Lang Wooton or Allsop & Co. for commercial sites. Barnard Marcus and Willmotts are best for residential plots. A third method might be to approach land buyers who advertise in the property journals and offer them the parcel. On occasion you may be able to structure a deal whereby you are bought out but retain a carried interest in the total ultimate profits from the development. In this way you stand a chance of enjoying a percentage of a tremendous gain, while simultaneously receiving hard cash down, so cancelling most of your risk.

Who generally owns land? The major organisational property owners have a high proportion – groups such as British Rail, BT, the Church, the Waterways Authority, local councils, and mining groups such as Amey Roadstone (now ARC, part of Consolidated Goldfields). The land register is closed to unauthorised persons, but is to be opened in 1989/90. Until then, essentially the only way to discover who owns land is to be in possession of the title oneself! There are various devious ways of getting some information via the rating authorities, but they are not foolproof, and may only lead to a managing agent. But local homework cold calling among neighbours can reveal much, and is to be recommended.

Underused land is widespread in Britain, and does little good to anyone. The shortage of useful new space means full exploitation of wasteland is a benefit to the community. Unlocking such parcels can be hugely lucrative. Just one successful deal can return such grand profits as to be worth 6 or 9 months patient effort trying to buy the land and dealing with awkward planning authorities. It is an area where many fortunes are still to be made, and beginners can strike lucky.

14

Save on Tax

There are two significant tax benefits to owning your own home. Firstly, the interest repayments on any mortgage up to £30,000 on the property receive tax relief. Secondly, any profits made on the sale of the home are capital gains tax free. These benefits only apply to one's principal private residence. Until the 1988 budget, interest on loans taken out to improve one's home also enjoyed tax relief, but this is now being phased out.

It therefore makes sense to keep a mortgage up to £30,000 on your main home. For a 40% taxpayer with an 11% repayment mortgage, this is worth £1,320 a year. You should also elect to choose the property yielding the highest capital gain as your principal private residence when you move. Whether you are classed as a property trader or not, everyone is permitted by the Inland Revenue to move from time to time, and the saving on this is clearly high, given the new 40% capital gains tax level. Many people live in and do up homes simultaneously as an occupation, buying and selling perhaps once a year. You should not rely upon getting away with this over an extended period of time – say any more than five years. The Inland Revenue will become aware of your "trade" and start taxing your annual lump-sum profit as income. It has been known for non-married couples to live in a house owned by one of them, then move into a house owned by the other and repeat the process.

If you have serious ambitions to launch a career as a property developer, you should consider which type of corporate vehicle to use from a legal and tax point of view. The new lower 40% top rate of income tax means the old advantages of incorporating your activities into a limited company and paying yourself a salary as a director are less compelling. The problem often with companies is that you pay corporation tax on the profit made by the company, and then income tax on any receipt by way of dividend. This can be avoided by setting up a simple trust company. There are costs to be saved acting as a sole trader in not needing an audit and a filed tax return at companies house. However, companies offer considerable protection against creditors and your liability in many instances is limited. Of course in practice bank managers in the initial stages will invariably demand personal rather than company guarantees for loans, and major suppliers will want prepayment for a new company. There is the apparent credibility of a Ltd Co structure, but sophisticated commercial individuals are not fooled, since they know shelf companies can be bought for £100. If you are unlikely to undertake more than one or two property deals a year which will in total make less than £50,000, do not incorporate. If you have ambitions greater than this, use a limited company.

If you work with partners, form a limited company and take shares unless you know them extremely well. In the latter case, you can seek some protection in the event of a dispute with a formal partnership agreement. But ultimately you are jointly and severally liable for the partnership debts. This means that if you both lose money on a deal, your partner could run off and you would have to pay off the entire amount owing. So think carefully before charging ahead with a little-known acquaintance on risky projects borrowing large amounts of money using personal guarantees.

If you buy and sell the occasional property which is not an exempt transaction, you may simply class any profit as a capital gain, but ordinarily you will not be able to charge expenses of a recurring nature against the gain for tax purposes. Previously the lower (30%) CGT level made such a system more attractive, but with lower income tax levels following Lawson's 1988 Budget such benefits are nullified. If you channel your property activities through a limited company, you will pay Corporation Tax on any unfranked income. The current rate is 35% for larger companies, 25% for smaller companies – those where the profits are less than £100,000. Marginal relief is applicable between the limits of £100,000 and £500,000. As a professional property trader and developer – self employed – (even if part-time) you can deduct all costs connected with a deal from the gross profit before arriving at the taxable profits. This can include a proportion of such items as car costs, phone and other expenditures made in carrying out dealing activities. The taxman will expect you to keep proper books of record, with retained receipts, invoices and records of sales. Your accountant will use these documents to draw up an annual set of accounts consisting of a trading statement and balance sheet. Brown envelope style cash payments to agents and runners for really sweet deals (while probably being illegal) can cause problems for both you and him and should be avoided. VAT is not chargeable on properties, and since you only make such exempt supplies you do not have to register. However, if you wish to build new properties or refurbish listed buildings then the cost is VAT exempt and it can be worth registering to reclaim VAT on builders' work and materials.

Expenses incurred on property let out can be charged against profits. This includes interest on borrowings taken out to buy or improve the rental property. More obvious deductable expenses are rates, maintenance and repairs, and any managing agent's fee. Rental income is classed as investment income and a special section is devoted to it on your tax return. It is normally taxed under Schedule A. However income from furnished lettings is taxed under Schedule D Case VI. Tax is payable on 1st January in the tax year in which the property income is due and is subject to the basic (25%) and higher (40%) rates of tax in the same way as earned income. You can claim an additional 10% deduction of the rent for tax purposes when letting furnished property to allow for wear and tear. Details of your UK property income should be entered in your tax return under "Property in the UK" in the INCOME section of the IIP and II forms.

The overall rule of thumb is that investment properties should be held by individuals and dealing properties by companies. The relatively low rate of tax now ruling in the UK ought to suggest that you pay all the tax fairly owing, since the burden is not great, even at the 40% band. The consequences of not paying tax can be severe, since the taxman charges onerous rates of interest on unpaid tax and will eventually punish persistent offenders – ask Lestor Piggott!

15

Invest in Farmland

Farmland has been a depressing investment in recent years. In the last three years it has declined by around 40% in value, compared with a steady climb in value over the previous 20 years. This recession in agricultural land values – compared to resilience in most commercial and residential property values in much of Britain – reflects the different market forces at play. Farms are not simply accommodation to work and live in; they are valued as businesses which generate crops or animal products. And in recent years the rising surplus of such foods within the EEC has seen declining farm profits and consequently falling revenues. Only massive subsidies under the Common Agricultural Policy have prevented widespread bankruptcies among farmers. But good residential farms in the area south west of London rose by up to 30% in value in 1987.

It is estimated that at lease 20% of cereal acreage is redundant to market demand. With ever more efficient farming methods, the over-production of crops within the EEC continues to rise. The business of farming is now wholly dependent on quota systems and central government pay-outs. Large farming combines benefit significantly at the expense of smallholders from this uneconomic structure. As a property market agricultural land breaks down into three sectors: commercial farms where the profitability of farming is the dominant feature; farms and estates where the property is a place to live rather than a business to be run; and the third sector of investment property let out to tenants. Broadly 60% of farmland is owner-occupied, while the rest is tenanted. Essentially one should either look at owning farmland to rent out, or owning and farming as a business. Farming has clearly not been as good a business as owning farmland (until the last few years) to judge by the 23 fold increase in farmland value from 1946 to 1978 against the mere 9 fold growth in net farm income during the same period.

Historically most farms have been family owned, either by modest smallholding farmers or much richer (often titled) country gentry. In the past farms were financed by internal funds or the Agricultural Mortgage Corporation, which lent on a fixed interest basis over 60 years, restricted to two-thirds of the farm's value. Nowadays banks lend on much more flexible terms. Around 0.2% of the total bank of agricultural land is turned over to urban or forestry uses annually. The Ministry of Agriculture has to be consulted on any planning applications turning over more than 4 hectares of agricultural land for development. Most of the development occurs at the urban fringe, where smallholdings have been fragmented and such problems as vandalism and tresspass threaten the viability of livestock farming. Frequently farmers have deliberately allowed patches to deteriorate in order to achieve successful planning, by arguing that the farm is unworkable. Such situations can offer fantastic uplifts in value, with agricultural land fetching perhaps £5,000 an acre, and good South-East housebuilding land with planning consent worth perhaps £300,000 an acre.

The bright spot within farm values has been the soaring worth of residential farm buildings. Farmhouses have climbed in value as fast as most desirable country property, and the potential to convert redundant barns etc. into luxury homes has not been lost on many farmers. Even if a structure is derelict and has been unlived-in for many years, local planning authorities may not be able to object if you replace it with a new building. They might demand a replacement barn, for instance, to be erected when an old one is demolished and replaced with a prized cottage, but inexpensive metal structures often suffice. You can assess perhaps whether outbuildings might have redevelopment potential, but it needs an expert to value the entire holding. A land surveyor should be hired to prepare a full report on any proposed purchase. This will include details of the soil, drainage, access, water supply, and how suitable the arrangement of the holding is for farming. If you are looking at the purchase as purely a break-up deal, such considerations will not worry you, but you ought to be in a position to decide whether it is an economic proposition as a farm if your planning applications fail.

Clever buyers in the last couple of years have bought in the West Country. The M4 has opened up the counties of Avon, Wiltshire, Gloucestershire and Somerset, and BR's Inter-City 125 has speeded travelling to Bath. Price inflation there is 25% per annum and likely to continue strong. Devon too is seeing good growth, being particularly popular as a retirement area. The West Midlands is now beginning to take off, and astute buyers would be looking to invest there for a two year view.

Over 80% of Britain's land area is in agricultural use, a ridiculously high percentage given the overcrowded nature of our island. The inconvenience of farming in much of the UK, and the potential cheapness (taking away EEC restrictions) of many imported foods compound the folly of such a land allocation. The disastrous collapse in farmland values in the last couple of years has stopped, and longer term investors could do worse than acquire marginal plots close to growing urban areas. It is worth noting that wily property traders like Mountleigh have bought over 20,000 acres of farmland in the last year or so. Nevertheless, farmland will remain essentially an investment rather than dealing situation. The inevitable increase in urbanisation should encroach and force up the value of such holdings many times over a few years. Farming as a business requires much hard work and considerable resources and knowledge if one is to be successful on anything but a small scale. Its economic viability relies upon layers of subsidies and regulations which might be removed at some future point. In a fully free market many of Britain's farms would shut down. But at present it provides a healthy living to many rich farmers, who also benefit from occasional windfall property development profits. First move for those interested is to contact an agricultural agent.

16

Develop Timeshare Resorts

A timeshare is the right to the exclusive use of a property for a certain period of the year, usually in perpetuity but occasionally for a fixed term. Timeshare developments have mushroomed everywhere from the Algarve to the Scottish Highlands, and in the process have acquired a very mixed reputation. Not only have unscrupulous developers overcharged for these two or three week chunks, they have oversold them, and in some cases gone bust, carrying the public's money with them.

The concept ought to make sense, in that ordinary people who could not afford to buy outright a fine foreign villa can pay say one 20th of the overall cost and enjoy the property for that percent of the year. But there are many potential pitfalls. The other timeshare investors may not treat the unit with respect, and it might deteriorate faster than a sole owner home. The secondary market for those who want to change has proved deeply disappointing, and people have been obliged to keep their share for ever, despite becoming bored with the resort. Initial buyers frequently pay too much (the total of a full year's sales equalling several times the property's true worth) and have lost money on a sale. Service charges can be painfully high. Hidden covenants can prove traps – some even specify that only the named buyer may occupy the property – even his family are forbidden to use it! Other developments do not sell partial ownership of the property, but simply the right to use it, while ownership remains vested with the developer. If the developer then goes broke – you lose your money!

We do not believe much money can be made as a buyer

of a timeshare. But there are considerable opportunities for developers of these schemes, as the idea is attractive to the average person. So far most projects have been built in Spain and Portugal, but there is potential for apartment blocks everywhere from the South Coast of Britain to Eire. Not only can you yield more per property sold if it is a timeshare development, but you can sell to a much larger market than if you were pushing whole villas. Most buyers would not bother raising a mortgage (banks and building societies will not lend against them anyhow) for say £10,000 or whatever a timeshare might cost. Whereas they would have to in order to buy a Spanish apartment – which might cost £70,000 – and UK building societies are loathe to advance money on such propositions.

Many major property developers have become investors in timeshare schemes – Barratt, Costain and Wimpey are big players, for instance. In 1987 over 40,000 families bought into timeshare projects. The Timeshare Developers Association is trying to clear up the poor image of hard-sell and unhappy buyers. Total British sales have now topped £250 million, and many sales organisations and developers have done well. In other countries the developments have been even more staggering – the business is worth some $1.5 billion in America, and in total around the world 1.5 million people have bought a timeshare unit.

Timeshare developments are expected to be high quality. They should offer a much better standard of accommodation than conventional self-catering units. They ought to be close to convenient transport and beach/ski facilities, and near airports when necessary. There should be above-average communal facilities such as pools, games rooms, laundrettes etc. Maintenance and servicing of rooms should be organised centrally and planned well beforehand. The type of investment required for such developments is likely to be huge, and the best bet for a beginner is to buy into a conversion project as an investor, learn the ropes and then later start one on their own.

America would seem to be an excellent area to start. With the US$ fairly weak against the UK pound, property in many parts of the US – Florida, California, etc – is not expensive and of a high standard by British measures. The common language is clearly a strong selling point, as is the fantastic range of facilities out there. Already huge US groups like Marriott and Hilton are involved in timeshare projects, while Disney is likely to start soon.

The possibility also exists of making a continuing profit out of running the projects on an ongoing basis. But the initial capital net is the real attraction to developers – quite often you can make 300% more than if you were simply selling a conventional unit to locals.

17

Contrary Investment in Property

It pays when investing to avoid the crowd. You should give close attention to what they do however, and at the appropriate moment – do the opposite. Following these tactics has paid off enormously over centuries in the stock market, which has watched booms and busts come and go regularly. Property tends to be a more stable asset than shares, but speculators can still get hurt – as they did in the 1974 property crash. It is therefore well worth bearing in mind the key contrarian signs to watch out for, and act accordingly.

The major factor leading to sliding property prices is spiralling interest rates, combined with a credit squeeze. High borrowing costs mean developers cannot afford to keep property trading stock. Meanwhile expensive mortgages and the withdrawal of bank lending lead to a scarcity of buyers. The recession, which is likely to follow a squeeze on credit, forces property-owners to sell at distressed prices. Simultaneously, cutbacks in businesses may push up office vacancies and force down office rents. So heavily-mortgaged commercial property developers are unable to meet their interest repayments, and default. Hence foreclosure properties become more common.

The key characteristics which signal the bottom of a price dive (and the time to start looking to buy) are:

- Housing starts at a low: a recession will force house-builders to cut back, and so supply will diminish. Demand will take a while to recover, but will result in new home supplies, leading to an imminent pressure on prices.

- News reports focusing on a distressed property industry: reading and hearing about unemployed and bankrupt builders and developers are all signs that it's time to start buying.
- High vacancy rates: if plenty of office space is unlet, and flats left unsold, then it is the time to start picking up deals.
- Estate agents offering juicy-sounding deals: when agents start phoning you and suggesting properties, instead of you phoning them for properties, then you can be sure they're getting desperate because properties aren't selling and they aren't making a living.

The opposite characteristics should scare you away from property investment and suggest the market is topping out:

- Complete property amateurs making "Loadsamoney" in property: when virtually everyone is turning into a developer, then it is time to move into a different business. If it is really that easy to make money, then the bubble is about to burst.
- Newspaper articles on a booming property market: if too many observers claim the market seems to be rising endlessly, then jump ship.
- Too easy money: if the banks are so eager to lend money (along with building societies) that they are falling over themselves, then they will make mistakes, and perhaps retrench severely when these errors come to light – when interest rates climb, perhaps?
- Low vacancy rates in offices, and few flats for sale: if all available property is snapped up by flush buyers paying over the odds, then the market is too hot. Minimal vacancies in offices encourage building sprees, which inevitably lead to gluts of space a few years down the road.
- Too many estate agents: when every other new shop is an estate agent, and they all seem to be making money, then something is rotten.

Conflicting signals are being transmitted at present. While London's office and housing markets show certain overdone symptoms, the regions – especially the Midlands and the North-West demonstrate clear signs of an upturn from the bottom. The important points to bear in mind if you feel a bust is around the corner are –

  (i) Don't over borrow – make sure you have equity in a property.
 (ii) Buy good quality property in good locations, where values will hold.
(iii) Buy cheaply in the first place – in that way values can fall and you're still not hurting.

18

Build Hotels

Hotel developments in the right area can be fantastically profitable. Property sages say that in some locations a freehold site with permission for a hotel is worth one and a half times as much as a site with office consent. The popularity of Britain as a tourist resort has lead to a boom for many hoteliers and big construction programmes all over the country. Forecasts predict that the lodging industry will continue to prosper, and that demand for hotel accommodation in many districts will carry on rising. There are therefore still fortunes to be made building or converting hotels.

Hotel properties have different characteristics to most commercial real estate. The key to success is management and the maximisation of room occupancy. Even if the location is right, a hotel can fail through poor service. Nowadays hotels derive income from a diverse spread of clients and activities. There are both holidaymakers and business travellers; and tours and conference and exhibition business. And there are spin-off profit generators such as function rooms for hire, restaurants, bars, and even sports clubs. The mix of facilities desired and possible should be carefully considered, weighing up the type of location served. Hotels are needed in coastal resorts, airports and historic cities and near conference centres. Once you have assessed your main source of business, try to develop an appropriate facility.

Large hotels are expensive undertakings. A 50 room building in a provincial town might cost £2 million to develop from scratch. Even budge hotels will cost between £20,000 and £35,000 per bedroom to build. Planners can be rigorous in their demands for parking spaces and district surveyors and safety officers are fussy about the quality of construction and services. It often makes much more sense to buy existing hotels and refurbish or extend them. But they do not come cheap. Price inflation for hotel properties in prime locations such as Central London has raged at over 20% per annum over the last five years. A London flagship hotel may well cost up to £250,000 per room to buy owing to the limited opportunities. Moreover, recent surveys suggest a shortage of 30,000 bedrooms in London by the mid 1990s, and much of this demand is likely to remain unsatisfied. Major groups such as airlines, holiday charter firms, the brewers and Grand Metropolitan and Trusthouse Forte have sunk many millions into the industry. The initial operating yield (pretax profit assuming 80% occupancy) on a hotel investment can be as low as 5% – rivalling a first-class office investment, and requiring much more management. But demand from major buyers is still rising. US operators like Inter-Continental and Holiday Inn are still expanding, while Ladbroke, now owners of Hilton outside the US, are significant investors in the field. As a developer you can negotiate a deal whereby a major operating partner will help fund the entire project, and you retain a carried interest in the completed investment which they manage. For your part you must find the deal and secure all consents necessary.

There are new sorts of hotels which are providing handsome opportunities to developers. Motels on major motorways and roads are springing up to offer budget accommodation to business travellers and enroute holiday-makers. The Channel Tunnel has created considerable activity in the South East, while new airports are an important spur. Finance for hotels is often put up by the largest institutional investors such as insurance companies. Since the risk is greater, so interest rates can be higher than for office or retail developments. For larger projects a lender will want a firm commitment from a well-known operating company before putting up the cash. In certain areas grants are available and help from Tourist authorities, in order to encourage that industry.

There are significant overseas opportunities in hotel development. Countries such as Greece, Portugal and Spain have been a goldmine for many developers who have capitalised on those countries' popularity as a holiday destination. Turkey is now a hotel development hotspot, and the weakness of local currency and cheapness of construction costs there have only enhanced its attractions. America has a huge wealth of motels priced from £200,000 upwards and hotels from $400,000 and there are many for sale at any time. The market there is very competitive for hotel operators and guests are demanding, so expect to work exceedingly hard if you wish to make a fortune in that business.

Careful planning and design go into making a profitable hotel. Common services to rooms must be designed for maximum efficiency. Furnishings should appear smart but must be hard-wearing. Public rooms should be accessible from the street. Kitchens must be immediately accessible to lifts to ensure efficient room service. Acoustics and sound-proofing are areas of concern and require sound specialists. Nowadays pools and sports facilities are often needed in addition to standard bar and restaurant services.

Hotels are generally investments for larger players with considerable property experience and resources. They have the potential to yield higher returns than practically any other form of property development, but sensible opportunities are infrequent and usually need plenty of funds and lots of time. Follow typical industry values on a per bedroom basis, but remember that many variables should also be taken into account, such as tenure, trade, location, facilities, local competition and standards. If you do venture into these waters, take a rich and capable partner – preferably a recognised operating group.

19

Dealing in New Homes

The rampant price inflation in new homes in the South East over recent years has created new money-making opportunities. While in some cases it is possible to make significant profits with little money down, the risks are high. Virtually all housebuilders and flat developers like to pre-sell most of the units – if not all. This helps cashflow for them and ensures the success of the scheme, and the more flats in a development sold, the easier it is to sell the remainder. In order to encourage buyers, developers offer two things: (i) a discounted price; and (ii) a system whereby buyers can put down a deposit of perhaps just 10% with the balance only payable when the project is finished.

Most speculative home schemes in London and the home counties have sold like hot cakes to keen first-time and richer buyers. If the project takes a year from sale of home by deposit to completion, inflation might well have increased the value of each unit by 20%. Taken together with the initial discount, the return on actual money invested can be phenomenal – if you can sell the building at what you believe is a "market" price.

As an example, take a 3 bed Essex house being sold for £90,000 off plan (a 10% reduction on the then market worth of £100,000). A 10% deposit, or £10,000 cash, has to be put down to secure the home. The house is finished a year later, during which homes have appreciated by say 15% (let's be conservative) – it is therefore worth £115,000. The owner immediately sells it and makes a gross profit of £25,000 – perhaps £22,000 after interest, legal and resale costs. This works out as a 110% return on the original investment – after just one year! The leverage effect of the deposit operates massively in your favour – assuming prices are rising and demand is healthy.

The magical thing about this game is that few resources are required. Most banks will give you an overdraft of around £10,000 – with some margin to pay off interest etc. during the year's wait. Gold credit cards are the usual route to such a facility. The ideal move is to sell the property (or contract) just ahead of completion, so that the ultimate buyer has to put up the full 100% and pay the stamp duty, rather than you. But if the value really has risen comfortably, an understanding bank manager will probably lend you the completion monies on a bridging finance basis with the house as security – until you sell it. All this manipulation does however cost money, both in arrangement fees and interest, and these ancilliaries should be taken into account when assessing the overriding profitability of the deal.

There are quite considerable risks in this wheeze. If you do not have the money to complete a year or so down the road, you lose your deposit and could get sued for any losses the developer suffers. If property prices fall – or even remain flat – the profits are miserly. In Docklands several wide-boys from the City burnt their fingers badly after Black Monday. They had bought by deposit several substantial and expensive flats each, planning on turning the contract before completion at a tidy profit. But the Crash took the wind out of sales of these flats, and in some cases saw the City wizz kids sacked – and losing money on the stock market! Not only were the flats unlikely to rise in value as planned – they cannot be sold – developers are enforcing the completions. This switchback has led to some crippling losses. In some cases individuals have been broken financially.

The lessons to be learnt from this debacle are simple. Do not commit yourself to purchases which you cannot possibly afford to complete; do not undertake more than one "futures" home purchase within a specific project; and avoid the most speculative schemes, which are not assured of success. Basic housing for first-time buyers, rather than City yuppies, is perhaps a safe market. One bedroom flats, for instance, are almost always saleable. Quite a good way of judging the eventual marketability is to look at the property as if you were going to live in it. Would you want to buy it to live in? How would it compare in value with similar properties? As a safeguard, you should also investigate just how lettable the property is if you are forced to hold it for a while.

To learn about these opportunities, scour the local papers for details of new developments. Keep your eyes open for any projects near you, and go and investigate when sales start. There are several glossy magazines published monthly which feature exclusively the various housebuilders' projects around the country. Or phone the head sales offices of the major housebuilders directly – they can point you to the projects likely to come on stream in future, so that you can register interest before the full selling programme is underway – and the crowds build up. The more demand for the homes, the better will be the immediate resales. Avoid buying properties in projects where demand seems non-existent – it's best not to be quite first in the queue, to ensure there are others to pass the home on to!

20

Buying US Property

North America represents the most valuable and highly developed real estate market on earth. The recent weakness of the US dollar against Sterling represents a worthwhile opportunity for UK property investors to enter this market. But since exchange rates are likely to continue to be volatile, and prospects for the $ look mixed, it is well worth while matching borrowing and assets – i.e., borrowing money in America in dollars to buy there.

The rules of the game in America are very different. It is far more realistic to think in terms of borrowing 100% of the cost of a property – re-financing is commonplace. Smaller buyers should only consider residential property initially, since commercial real estate in a minefield for the amateur. Moreover, since private residential landlords still thrive in most areas of the US, residential income property can be a sensible option.

Real estate brokers (as they call estate agents) are far more regulated in the US. They have to pass exams and become licensed and members of local associations of realtors. They derive a far higher commission – perhaps 6% – than their UK counterparts, but undertake much of the work involved in conveyancing (or settlement as it's called in America). You will get better service from a US broker, but also a high pressure sell – so beware. Most simple residential purchases and sales do not require the services of an attorney or lawyer, but you may choose to use one if it is your first US deal and you are worried about being ripped off. It is worth bearing in mind however that since brokers are more regulated, both by state and federal law, than is the case in the UK, they are bound to treat both sides fairly – although they essentially act for the seller.

Once you have made an offer, be prepared to put 3% of the price down as a form of deposit. This will be held in escrow until the purchase is closed (completed). Purchase is normally subject to such conditions as a satisfactory inspection (structural survey) and financing. More thorough warranties as to such things as termite infestation, air conditioning, plumbing etc. are offered than is usual in the UK. Purchase is normally also contingent upon obtaining a clean title and if necessary the sale of another home. Title search companies undertake the equivalent of local searches and offer guarantees.

The cost of buying is much higher in America. While you will not have to pay a lawyer a half percent fee as here, there are other costs which add up to perhaps 4% of the total bill. These include a fat fee to the escrow company, the title search fees, and significant mortgage fees. This latter charge will include an appraisal fee, a loan origination fee, and mortgage insurance. But mortgages are usually dealt with direct by the broker rather than via a specialist mortgage broker, so no fee is payable to a third party.

Financing is hugely more sophisticated than in Britain. Life assurance policies rarely accompany mortgages, and interest rates are often lower in America, so carrying costs of property are lower. Since plenty of residential income property is owned by private individuals, multiple mortgages are common. Lenders often have inducements such as lower interest rates to first-timers – but these rates normally only last 3 months. Since traditionally fixed interest rate mortgages have been the norm, they are still widely available, at perhaps one and a half percent above variable rate mortgages. For those concerned about climbing interest rates, they might be a safe bet. Normally mortgages are for 30 years, but 15 year mortgages are possible. The providers of funds are primarily savings and loan associations, organisations similar to building societies. They are however different in that they are mostly bankrupt, although the government provides depositors with insurance. It is often possible to have the vendor finance the purchase of a property for an initial period of perhaps 3 years. In these cases, "no money down" is possible – although risky. Clearly there is no UK tax relief on principal private residence loan interest. But all interest is tax-deductible under US law, a useful saving if you enter the rental property market.

The two types of flat or apartment are condos or co-ops. Condos (short for condominium) are a little like flying freeholds, with the common parts and exterior structure owned by all the residents of a block communally. A co-op is a building owned by a company in which you buy shares allocated to a particular apartment, as well as a proprietory lease for the unit. Co-ops typically have an underlying lease on the entire property, so monthly payments include both interest and overall building maintenance charges. Co-ops are less frequent and offer less appreciation to investors and are being bought up and sold off as condo blocks. Both are largely found in major cities rather than suburbs, since the great American concept of owning your own house is still strong – and there is plenty of room in America compared to Britain.

Tenants tend to have considerably less security of tenure than in the UK. While some rents are regulated, they are far nearer market rents than most UK registered rents – except in certain cities like New York. Evicting tenants sometimes requires payment of a compensation fee, which might run to say $3,000 at most. There is normally available for sale rental property which shows a modest positive cashflow from day one after financing – excluding management charges. Often the best bargains are from distressed sellers or foreclosure properties. Many would-be millionaires try to make fortunes in real estate in America and over-gear themselves, and it can be highly profitable taking advantage of their problems.

The key to making real estate profits in the US is knowledge of the complex financing techniques and familiarity with the market you are entering. Each state has different economic pressures and laws. You will need to find a trustworthy ally over there – perhaps a broker, possibly an attorney – who is in a position to offer advice and contacts. But you only have to read Donald Trump's book "The Art Of The Deal" to realise what huge sums can be made from American property.

21

Run a Letting Agency

Peter Rachman started in property by running a letting agency in Bayswater in the 1950's. Don't let that put you off, however. Although there are plenty of rogues who cheat both tenants and landlords, there are also a great many straight letting agents who earn considerable sums and provide a needed service.

Letting agents act for landlords in finding tenants for flats and houses. They generally "manage" the property for them too; for the combined service, a fee of 15% of rentals received – plus all out-of-pocket expenses – will typically be charged. Some cowboys might undercut this percent, but will in consequence tend to offer a cut-rate service with it. Letting agents are not permitted by law to charge a fee to prospective tenants, although some try to get round this by selling flat rental lists. The buyers are generally desperate foreigners or students, who don't know any better. Technically such agents can be prosecuted.

The job itself is to find suitable tenants for the home owner. A good deal of discretion should be employed, since the Landlord & Tenant and Rent Acts are minefields, and dubious tenants two-a-penny. Usually the agency will offer the landlord advice about the type of letting agreement to draw up – whether it be some form of Company let or Holiday Letting. Letting agents usually prefer the former, feeling that corporate bodies tend to be reliable about paying bills and keeping properties in good order. Moreover, companies do not have any security of tenure which allows them to remain in occupation once the tenancy has expired, although they can apply to the rent officer for a fair rent to be registered.

As a letting agent you will supply standard forms drafted by your lawyer for use by your clients. You can charge around £50 for this. It is essential that any competent letting agent has a good knowledge of the law, especially the Rent Acts.

Letting agents advertise through a shop-front and newspaper classifieds. The requirement for retail space is less great than when selling property – the limited supply of rental accommodation ensures the tenants come to you – via the phone. So a simple office above a shop can suffice. You will have to attempt to find flats and houses to let. Other than press adverts, many agents now do letter box drops in appropriate areas, or form a joint venture with a conventional agent. You handle all letting enquiries generated through their outlet(s). In return you give the selling agent a proportion of your 15% fee – perhaps one third, depending on the level of business he supplies. Your overheads should be minimal, and really success is guaranteed if you can find a healthy number of decent properties to let at reasonable prices. You should ensure a professional service is provided to your client – the landlord – and they can provide a juicy income stream for a tiny effort for years.

Very often property owners use letting agents because they have to go away or do not have the time or expertise to handle the letting procedure. As a letting agent, you should have sound applicants waiting for the right sort of property, and you should know exactly what rent to suggest your client charges. You ought to be in a position to find suitable tenants who can pay more than the tenants a landlord alone would find. It pays letting agents to canvass organisations who have people needing accommodation – such as hospitals with little space for nurses, universities, and foreign companies with visiting personnel.

You must take up references on tenants and extract deposits. You will take a list of the home's contents and the state of decoration – you should be able to charge around £20 for this service. During a tenancy you will hand over keys and collect rents and ensure the tenants are keeping the house in reasonable order – a regular inspection will be required, and reports sent to the owner. Repairs and servicing must be handled by the letting agent, and tenants will complain to you if the roof leaks or the washing machine breaks down. These tasks are dull to cope with, and it pays to have reliable maintenance staff contacts to undertake repairs that crop up. The agent should advertise a tie-up with a local solicitor so prompt action can be confidently recommended to the client in the event of non-payment of rent, breakages, squatters etc.

Letting agents normally as a matter of course ask whether properties are mortgaged, and require the owner to alert the building society or bank about the letting. They also as a safeguard deduct as a normal procedure the standard rate of income tax from the rent receivable, since the Inland Revenue are in frequent contact with them regarding landlords and rental payments. But remember to remind your client that letting and management fees are deductible as an expense for tax purposes. A letting agent might be liable for tax if the owner does not pay. Some agents offer various forms of insurance against tenants damaging property or failing to pay rents – these are underwritten by major insurance companies, and clearly the landlord pays extra for these security blankets. Letting and management agents are expected to deal with tenants who fail to pay or cause trouble as a matter of course. Occasionally licenced bailiffs are required, and a Court Order needed to remove difficult individuals. This should be rare, since a good agent should not have permitted such tenants to take up residence in the first place.

22

Choose the Right Location

Jack Cotton is often credited with the line which lists the famous three essentials for success in property: "location, location, location." He meant that one was always right to buy if a property was in a prime site – almost whatever the cost or conditions in the market. That may well be true, but is of less relevance to smaller property developers than to a tycoon like Cotton or his partner Clore. Dealers in modest residential property and part-time investors cannot afford to purchase the finest located buildings or land. With central City of London rents upwards of £60 a square foot for office space, and such investments yielding as little as 4%, only the biggest players can participate in the game. So how does Cotton's advice apply to the up-and-coming developer?

The important point to remember about property locations is not that only the best is good enough – but that you must be fussy. You should only buy locations which are good value. That means you can pay top dollar for smart street houses, but only bottom dollar for dumps. Never allow agents to fool you into thinking a secondary siting is worth a premium price, or that a rotten flat will sell for as much as a good one. Do not be afraid to deal in rougher neighbourhoods with lower rents and resales, so long as your price of entry is suitably low. Do however remember that for instance in London building costs in terms of labour and materials will not differ if you are working in Mayfair or Stockwell. Therefore, excluding interior specifications, you are likely to obtain a better return from time and money invested in building works in expensive locations than in inferior ones. And planning gains are similarly worth that much more in absolute terms when they apply to expensive districts. The key is really to buy cheaply in a good location. The individual cannot "lift" a location in price but can lift the value of an individual property.

Despite those drawbacks, there are positive sides to dealing in run-down areas. There is much more likelihood of finding older properties in need of renovation in tatty districts, and of coming across big houses which have the potential to be converted into flats. And cheaper districts will attract first-time buyers. These are the best pool of purchasers in the residential market, since they are never part of a chain, and can therefore buy without restrictions. They will also tend to want to live in studio, one and two bedroom flats – the major products of house conversions. And they also provide a strong upward pressure on prices – despite economic fluctuations. While existing houseowners can delay their move to a bigger home, first-time buyers are usually desperate to buy to escape the private renting nightmare.

Indeed it seems in London that those regions which have the most plentiful supply of cheaper houses and flats will climb in value more than most – as a percent of the value of the property. Thus once seedy areas such as Tooting and Holloway have seen prices rises of 35% plus per annum in recent years as first-timers flood in and gentrify. The gentrification process itself which areas undergo over a period of years produces something of a status change in the immediate residential environment. This effect boosts prices in addition to the general level of house inflation the overall area is experiencing.

There are sometimes clear pointers to indicate a lift-off in prices. New roads to help communication, new rail or air links to facilitate commuting, new factories or offices to give demand a shove, or new shopping or housing developments to clear slums or attract newcomers. Changes in local council policy can help streets or whole districts. The banning of curb-crawling in parts of Bayswater boosted prices, while severe restrictions on sex-shops led to rocketing flat prices in Soho. But the stripping away of the protective green belt around London might lead to tumbling house prices, as development of new homes intensifies dramatically. (But such a decision by the Secretary of State would also unlease massive inflation in farmland etc which could be used to build on.) Meanwhile the advent of the Channel Tunnel is pushing up prices rapidly at both putative ends. Planning departments can keep you informed about such developments. Rising crime, ethnic imbalances, and left-wing councils all damage house prices. Comparable London flats in different boroughs might receive rates bills of £250 (for a Tory council) and £1,250 (for a Labour council). The capital cost of an annual outgoing disparity of £1,000 is £10,000. Logically therefore a flat in the Labour borough should be £10,000 cheaper than a similar flat in the Tory-controlled borough. The poll tax will change this calculation somewhat.

Surveys are carried out periodically by newspapers and magazines to canvass views about areas on the rise. In recent years in Central London, Docklands and East London has been boom-town, and prices have soared by up to 50% a year. Already this bubble has burst with the October 1987 stock market crash, and prices have certainly fallen there, although the illiquidity of property means the awful truth is still to emerge for many Wapping studio proprietors. Unless you arrive at the start of a massive speculation binge such as that one, avoid them, since it is risky to buy purely in the hope that more gamblers will move in and buy you out. Telltale signs of an overheated area are too many estate agency practices with too many For Sale boards up, and too many yuppie homeowners making 30% in the first year after they've bought.

The South-East of England has experienced a sustained boom in house prices in the 1980s, while areas such as the North-East and Midlands have seen flat values. In 1982, the average Yorkshire house was worth

65% of an average London property; today the respective figure is just 36%. Clearly such a disparity is unlikely to last. The recovery now being felt in some of Britain's industrial heartland will certainly lead to greater employment and higher wages, and will be translated into a recovering homes market. The uplift in values is likely to be more dramatic in percentage terms, and of course the cost of entry is lower, with fine Newcastle homes for sale at one quarter the cost of an equivalent place in say Brighton or Oxford. And the competition from builders and developers in these areas in far less, while labour is cheaper and readily available, and grants from various bodies more widespread. Cunning developers are already making their presence felt.

Choosing your areas of operation is entirely a matter of taste. But it is apparent that some regions will see greater demand and inflation in land and property than others. It is possible to predict these trends, since they do not occur overnight, but happen over years, and are mainly caused by structural changes to the surroundings – be they a new motorway or a loosening of planning restrictions. It will pay to be aware of such events and take advantage of them.

23

Sell Without an Estate Agent

This section is primarily aimed at those house-owners who are willing to sell their own home without an agent. Dealers and developers may feel obliged to use agents. One reason to use agents is that such commission acts as a form of fee for finding deals. In other words, you instruct the agent who finds a piece of housebuilding land with the new home resales. Moreover, when dealing in commercial property, the sums involved are far larger and pitching to exactly the right tenant becomes crucial. Essentially, qualified commercial agents contribute far more to earn their fees, while residential agents on the whole add less.

The vast majority of residential property vendors instruct an estate agent to sell their home. The agent then markets the property and pockets a juicy brokerage commission. Rising house prices and increasing home ownership have attracted many to this lucrative trade. The number of estate agent shops has risen to at least 20,000 across Britain, and there are probably 4,000 in Greater London alone. They thrive on the 1% to 2% commission most agents charge – that's around £1,000 on a typical £50,000 sale. Some central London agents even charge 3%. Yet the job they do is comparatively easy, and requires virtually no qualifications or licence. A competent agent has the ability to position your property in the market place to achieve the greatest exposure to potential buyers. But they are not uniquely qualified. This section is about selling your flat or house without their services, and making (or saving) upwards of £1,000, while keeping complete control of the selling process.

Do-It-Yourself home selling needs serious intent and a

fair amount of work. The steps to take require only common sense and realism about prices. Firstly you should be sure you really want to sell – and that you have somewhere to move to; it usually doesn't pay to market your own house and get buyers excited before you're ready to vacate. If you're selling a property you don't live in, the process is more straight-forward, since there should be no chain – from your side, anyway.

1 Value The Property: collect every comparable piece of data about achieved sale prices of property as nearly similar as possible to yours. Use local papers, and go through every single local estate agent's property listing, trying to find properties of the same size in the same street. This should refine the idea you already have as to the market worth of your home. Always remember that just because a house has been listed as "£95,000", doesn't mean it will (or did) fetch that much. Then arrange for say two local agents to come and value the property. You will have to give them the impression that you intend to instruct them to sell it. It won't be necessary to lie, since if they are competitive they will do a free, simplistic valuation on a speculative basis, with no confirmation of any retention. Have them supply written valuations, for reference purposes and possibly to show interested buyers. Once you've collated all the relevant information, form a personal view as to the likely marketable worth of your home. Don't be greedy – remember any fool can become a well-informed judge of a particular locality's house prices, and will not over-pay. Try to pitch a value below that of the most ambitious estate agent valuation, since they often suggest a high price as a come-on to entice you to instruct them, knowing they ought to be able to sell it later at a lower price – still getting the commission. Moreover, any buyer knows you will be saving on estate agency fees, so will expect a slightly lower price in consequence. When selling your own home, you should push the fact that it is cheaper since you don't have to pay an agent.

116

2 Choose Your Marketing Tools: you need to expend effort to advertise well. You should determine which is the best local paper for property, and book well in advance say two consecutive modest display or classified adverts over two weeks. Be prepared to spend at least £75 on this – remember if one advert works, you have sold the property. If you have a smart house, you could try say The Sunday Times. London flat owners could use The Evening Standard. Avoid the national classified magazines and telephone sale services. Most buyers use the best local paper. Contact a local sign writing and erection service from the Yellow pages and rent or buy a smart board for the front of your home. These boards really do work, which is why agents love putting them up so much. When paying for this advertising, remember that agents frequently charge extra to advertise your home, on top of their usual commission. Use pretty accurate and economical language in your adverts; copy the style of the better agents' classified stuff. If you receive no interest from your advertising, you are either asking too much or putting adverts in the wrong place. Make sure you are in to answer the phone, or that you have an answering machine to take messages, when you receive advert responses.

3 Prepare Printed Particulars: draw up accurate measurements of the various rooms, and duplicate the page layout of more impressive agent details. If you can, draw a little plan of the flat/house. You can type these or have them set cheaply using the new desktop publishing systems for about £10. Use both sides of a single A4 sheet. Take a decent photo of your home – possible inside and out – and stick it on the original set of particulars. Then photocopy perhaps 40 sets initially, using a good machine like Xerox. You can use a colour photocopier to include proper copies of the photo, or get reprints of the photo to attach to each set of particulars. Use reasonably honest and helpful copy when writing about your home – don't fall for the estate agent hyperbole – but don't undersell the place. The particulars will be used principally to send out to prospective buyers who have phoned in response to your advert or board. Always include details of length of lease, rateable value, rates in the pound and rates payable, ground rent (if any), and service charge (if any). Put directions to get to the property on the instructions, and possibly a little map. Insist that viewing is by appointment only. Include a disclaimer that the property is being sold "subject to contract", and that the particulars do not form any part of the contract. It is possible that you may be liable for misrepresentation in respect of any particulars – try to be realistic!

4   Improvements: while living in a house or flat you may have allowed it to become a little shoddy. You may also have changed the interior arrangements to suit your own specific tastes. Generally houses which are being viewed by prospective purchasers should be as plain and simple as possible, with a minimum of ugly clutter and garish wallpaper or pictures. Remember that a serious buyer will normally have structural survey done, which may uncover defects which could put the buyer off or force you to introduce a discount. You are not advised to obstruct the surveyor's attempts to find faults as much as possible – e.g. cover rotting floorboards with nailed carpet, paint over dry-rot windows and wall cracks, recover damp ceilings, and prevent access to the attic, although people do. Generally redecorate if you feel the flat needs it, but think carefully before going to the expense of fitting new kitchens and bathrooms, say. You should only do this if you are selling an extremely fine residence, or if the existing bathroom and kitchen are terrible.

5   Viewing: always encourage phone respondents to adverts to look at the property – you might turn them into actual buyers. Try to be cooperative about viewing times. You will be stood up countless times by time-wasters, but don't get discouraged. When showing the property, stress the good points, and highlight convenient local facilities. Never mention bad features unless pressed – feign ignorance if possible. Don't directly lie. Use your best selling techniques, but try not to talk too much, or you may put the buyers off. Try to make sure they have the substance to do the deal – there are plenty of time-wasters around. Steer the conversation around to a close once they've seen the property. Be prepared to phone them afterwards to chase interest.

6 Agreeing The Deal: these days buyers all think an asking price will be discounted a little. You should only be willing under normal market circumstances to knock off 5%, although you may have to reduce your price further if you're desperate and the place won't sell. Remember to consider fixtures and fittings, and if you want to keep them and how much to charge for them if you don't. Once matters like this have been settled, and you have discovered whether they need a mortgage or have cash, swap solicitors' details and try to agree a proposed date of completion. As long as they have the wherewithal, first time buyers are better than buyers locked in a chain, since these dreadful property snakes can take many months to unravel.

Overall, selling your own house can be a fulfilling and money-saving exercise. Estate agents will rook you for VAT and anything else they can. When you market your house, you can highlight the best points and time it to suit yourself as far as possible. For the energetic, it is highly recommended.

24

Obtain a Mortgage

Most property experts agree their business has two aspects: the physical buildings and land; and their financing. Many of the most successful property entrepreneurs have had little feel for property, but have been talented at raising money and funding deals cheaply. If you can be sure of being able to borrow enough money at fine enough interest rates, you are half the way to making money.

Mortgages are funds extended which are secured upon a property. For residential property, building societies are the historic first source. But in recent years, an explosion of new lenders has generated a wide range of participants in the mortgage market – clearing banks, foreign banks, and specialist groups such as Household Mortgage Corporation and The Mortgage Corporation. Gone are the days when one had to have saved decent sums over a period of years with a building society in order to qualify for a mortgage. Nowadays anyone with a seemingly respectable set of references can walk in off the street and successfully apply for a mortgage.

There are various elementary features to consider about the mortgage one goes for. Firstly, should it be endowment or straight repayment? The former pays off the amount borrowed at the end of the mortgage term with the proceeds of an insurance policy – the latter pays off the mortgage in a mix of monthly interest and principal repayments. Repayment mortgages are cheaper if interest rates are above 11%; endowment mortgages should normally generate a surplus from the insurance policy at the end of the term. There are also now more sophisticated types, such as low start and fixed interest.

If you have a minimal income initially, the former is a good idea; the latter are worthwhile if you believe interest rates are going to climb.

Ensure that you obtain your legitimate tax relief on interest repayments. Under MIRAS (Mortgage Interest Relief At Source), you automatically receive the benefit on the first £30,000 of borrowed money interest repayments. The inland revenue will supply a form with any mortgage application, in order that you pay a net amount monthly. Clearly this benefit is only obtainable on one mortgage at a time.

Mortgage brokers are a new breed who have sprung up to shop around on behalf of mortgage seekers to get the most appropriate deal (or in some cases any deal!). They earn a living through the payments of commission by the life assurance companies which provide a life policy for the mortgagee. Do not pay them a commission yourself. They can sometimes smooth the passage of an application by being totally aware of the various qualifications each lender demands, and by chasing up the building society/bank etc for you. They may well in addition have details on the very latest types of mortgage on offer. Do however beware taking up a mortgage just because the presently offered rate of interest is extremely low – these do fluctuate. Rather obscure foreign banks have been known to offer low interest rates initially to attract business, and will then jack the rates up to well above the average.

If you have only a modest salary and tiny quantities of capital to put into a flat, you should definitely approach a mortgage broker. They are in business to earn commission, and will try their hardest to fix you a mortgage if it's humanly possible. The usual routine starts with a longish form from the potential lender. A status enquiry will be made as to the longevity of your employment and your salary. An accountant's letter will be expected if you are self-employed. Most lenders work on the principle on $3 \times$ annual income as to the loan extended. They will normally only lend around 2 × a joint income. This acts as another disincentive for people to marry – so far as property goes! The lender will commission a local chartered surveyor to visit the flat or house you want to buy for about £100. The surveyor will give the property a very brief valuation survey – on behalf of the bank remember, not you. This survey should not necessarily substitute for a full structural survey, if you feel one is desirable.

Few banks and building societies will now in practice lend 100% of the price of a property. Many play the trick of saying they will lend 100%, and then undervalue the property deliberately and lend only 100% of their undervaluation – forcing you to come up with the balance. Too many lenders of 100% mortgages suffered defaults and were unable to obtain their entire advance when they foreclosed, after all costs. If you consider yourself to be a potential defaulter – perhaps you're in a profession with uneven work spells, such as acting – you can insure against the failure to repay a mortgage. You pay a modest extra monthly premium, but it could be worth the relief.

When you apply for a mortgage you should discover what the lender's policy is regarding repayment. Some mortgage providers will charge a penalty if you try to repay the full amount within say two years. Often the sum will be three months' interest. If there is a likelihood of you having to redeem the mortage after a fairly short space of time, you should avoid these lenders. Avoid too lenders who prevent you getting a second charge on the property, if you wish to use the free slice of equity to borrow against.

There are several new types of mortgages available which brokers may try to sell you. Unit linked mortgages are similar to endowment in that repayments are saved, this time in unit trusts – they tend to be slightly higher risk, higher reward than conventional endowment policies. Pension mortgages use the tax exempt status of mortgages to help fund the repayments. Tax relief is available at 17.5% of earnings. Talk to a broker advertising in a magazine like The Mortgage Magazine for the latest offer; make sure the broker is a member of FIMBRA.

25

Buy Property on the Stock Market

Speculation in stocks rivals that in property as a mechanism for self-enrichment. Most big property spivs will trade on the stock market too. One way in which your growing knowledge of the property scene can be put to profitable use is through the measured purchase of selected property shares. Many surveyors and property professionals develop a far better understanding than average of the most able players among the quoted property companies, and add the shares to their portfolios.

The property sector is one of the largest on the London Stock Exchange and numbers at least 50 separate equities, both fully listed and USM. They range from dynamic so-called merchant developers and traders like LET run by the Beckwith brothers, to quiet residential investment companies like Reliable/Palmerston, part of the Freshwater empire. In addition there are housebuilders and building construction and contracting groups like Laing and AMEC. There are estate agency groups such as Connells and Sinclair Goldsmith. And there are other conglomerates with major property interests such as Ladbroke.

The buoyancy of City developments and new home markets has seen companies involved in these areas become very highly rated by the institutional investment community. Historically property companies have been valued on yields (dividend incomes) or assets rather than earnings per share multiples. But in the raging bull market of 1987 prior to the October crash, most property stocks ceased to trade at a discount to net assets, and there were flotations of several inferior companies. While

Black Monday sorted out some of the wild over-valuations with a thump, during the first months of 1988 property stocks have performed well. It seems the demand for high quality commercial space is still excellent thanks to the booming UK economy. And the prospects for residential newbuild seem undimmed by the crash.

The trick when investing in property companies is to use your field research. If you hear that a specific listed company has received permission for a huge new development, look into it and try to assess the impact the project will have on the overall group. Try to judge the timing of sales and the improvement in asset value and profits which will result. By the converse, if you see a big property group buying wildly at auction and paying too much for lots, make sure you don't own the shares. You could even consider buying a "put" option, a device which gives you the right (but not the obligation) to sell the given company's shares at the current market price up to three months' hence – for a premium. If you meet really superb developers from a new go-getting group, look into their company and buy some shares if you can see they're going places. Always try to rely upon your own research in matters like this, rather than trusting large investment sums to hearsay and rumours. Listen to the gossip, but try to verify it for yourself before taking the plunge with your cash.

Your market intelligence about sectors which are performing best will come in use when buying property company shares. In recent years the values of retail investments have soared, while industrial property has been fairly stagnant. The geographical bias has also been significant, with companies such as Wates City of London benefitting from the City financial services boom. Betting on takeovers can be a highly profitable pastime. There are still a number of older style property groups which seem vunerable to bids from the more aggressive newcomers like Speyhawk and Mountleigh.

Direct investment in individual shares is not the only

route into property via the stock market. One can buy unit trusts which have a specific bias towards property stocks, and hope the hired fund managers choose a suitably balanced bunch of property stocks. But be warned – there are one or two painful examples in this class – the two well-publicised London residential property unit trusts being examples. Both realised after the crash that clients desperately selling units would force the rushed liquidation of property investments – which would consequently fetch miserable prices in the period immediately post crash. The values of those particular units have slumped.

There are also investment trusts which have a bias towards UK property companies, but there are no authorised investment trusts investing directly in property in a big way. New schemes are being organised which will allow massive single buildings to be unitised, so that there will be joint ownership among many investors of a single real estate asset. This type of investment will allow you to buy into a particular project, but will carry the added risk that a more diversified property company share avoids. The market seems to be looking less kindly towards the property service companies such as estate agents and architects, and it would probably be best to leave such shares alone at present unless you like them particularly.

You will find the Property section in the weekly magazine The Investors Chronicle a worthwhile read, and Mike Foster's articles in the City section of the Evening Standard well informed. The Estates Times probably has the better coverage of stock market/property dealings. Various stockbrokers produce excellent research analysis of the various quoted property groups, with Rowe & Pitman probably the best. It could be well worth trying to get hold of their latest circular on a given company if you have serious interest in buying their shares.

The overall view of the property companies' prospects is that they should continue to outperform after the

October 1987 crash. Their powerful asset base, and the solid demand from tenants for most sorts of UK commercial property underlies improving profits. The major investing institutions, such as pension funds and insurance companies, are looking favourably towards real estate following the shock waves of the October 1987 stock market Crash. Their growing levels of investment will force down yields and boost values, so assisting the major property groups. Massive new developments such as the Kings Cross and Paddington Basin projects in London will generate substantial surpluses for the involved parties. Possible loosening of green-belt planning restrictions on residential developments will spur activity by the housebuilders such as Countryside, Bryant, Tarmac and Costain. A continued high level of bid activity is also anticipated, particularly in the wake of the 1988 budget changes to CGT prior to 1982, allowing some of the older groups to unlock significant gains at much lower tax rates. With luck and application you should make money buying quoted property stocks.

26

Become a Builder

The building trade is one of Britain's largest industries, and many construction companies are among the biggest of any in Britain – Wimpy and Trafalgar House to name but two. While construction and refurbishment work is a very different discipline to property dealing and development in terms of skills and finances, many builders make excellent developers. One of the finest ways of getting to know about property, the market, and buying, selling and renovating, is to start building yourself. Most property wheeler-dealers have engaged in the basic crafts of bricklaying, tiling, carpentry etc. at some stage. By undertaking each task one acquires a genuine understanding of quality of work and costs involved, and one can much better programme a series of works and organise men. And of course, it is always possible that construction itself will prove so lucrative that a separate entity will carry out those works alongside the property business itself.

While undertaking building work yourself you will discover how to deal with local planning departments, public health requirements, and the district surveyor. And in running your own building team – as many major developers like Speyhawk do – you deprive an outside builder of a profit and keep better control of the project. Indeed, such is the competition now for more straight-forward flat conversions in London that the developer's profit margin has been squeezed out, and only practising builders can extract reasonable returns after buying these development properties at market price. If you try to buy at auction, you will find yourself bidding against rough-and-ready types in dusty overalls. They are jobbing builders, who can afford to pay more, since they take the construction work margin.

The major problem when acting as prime contractor is labour. Building trade craftsmen and subcontractors can be a mercenary lot, and it is easy to over-pay for shoddy work. If you are actually going to be present on site supervising the entire job, you should hire individual self-employed labourers, and pay them by the hour – or day. Through the course of the work you will soon discover who is reliable and who is idle – keep the good ones and fire the no-hopers. Either the men themselves will help recommend further workers, or the local job centre or the local paper classified adverts will feature self-employed brickies, plasterers, carpenters etc. There are opportunities to hire men in the evenings and at weekends who are employed during normal working hours by big companies. Each trade commands a different rate, with electricians and plumbers being the most expensive craftsmen, and standard decorators being cheapest. Unless you are undertaking several largish jobs, you should subcontract and not directly employ. In this way you place the burden of tax and national insurance on your subcontractor's head, rather than obliging you to deal with it. Such subcontractors should technically have a tax exemption certificate, form 714. When you pay the subcontractor, you should be supplied with form 715 as a form of receipt – this should be sent to the tax inspector. Formal subcontractors will cost more, and you will have to pay VAT. To avoid going through this can be dangerous – Customs & Excise and the Inland Revenue can be rapacious debt-collectors, while many building trade cowboys are prosecuted each year for tax and VAT evasion. You will be able to complete the job for much less if you manage it this way, since you are paying each craftsman directly, without bearing the expense of a building firm's cut. Building labour has become very expensive in South-East England and London in particular, perhaps costing twice the rate payable in the North-

West and quite a number of cost-conscious developers have taken to recruiting labour from places like Tyne & Wear and Sheffield and bringing them to London. The craftsmen will often sleep in the building where the job is being carried out for much of the duration, and sometimes work harder and for much less than their London counterparts.

You will need materials supplied from builders' merchants. Get estimates for timber, plaster etc. from several nearby outlets and choose the firm with the best terms. You may be able to fix reasonable credit. The major DIY warehouses such as Homebase and Do It All are nowadays competitive in price too, and frequently open on Sundays – useful if you need to work weekends. You will also require a plant hire firm, to hire such equipment as scaffolding, ladders and welding tools. If you are to work on site yourself in an actual trade, you should buy your own tools. Subcontractors should bring all their own small tools. You may well need to hire a van to transport the various bits of equipment and bags of cement back and forth – it is worth considering the purchase of a second-hand vehicle if you are to regularly carry out works. To get trade discounts, you usually need the name of a firm and some form of letter heading.

Clearly if you enjoy undertaking building jobs and feel you do it well, then you can offer your service simply as a builder. This removes the risk of developing and not making a decent return, and can prove a sizable money-spinner. You will have to learn how to find and get on with clients and their architects, and how to price and charge for work – and extract the money. The highest margin work is small jobbing tasks for householders, such as re-rendering a flaking outside wall, but this type of smaller task can prove a headache to coordinate, and you need a steady flow to keep your men in work. Once you act for third party clients as a pure builder, then there are additional tax implications, since you will need exempt subcontract labour or to pay employees on a

PAYE basis, deducting National Insurance contributions. One further variant is to do joint ventures as a builder with developers. You, as builder, will stump up the building costs, the developer will contribute land, and the profits will be split according to some pre-agreed formula.

At the very least gaining hands-on experience of the building trade will help you understand development costings and the structure of buildings. If you enjoy seeing a personal job well done and running a building team then you will always do a job more cheaply and more precisely to your choosing when you totally supervise it. But the hours are long and the work exceedingly tiring, and it is unlikely to be nearly as profitable as spending time on the lookout for more property deals.

27

Get a Grant

Governments have made available via local councils considerable sums under the 1974 Housing Act to improve
the housing stock. These grants are available to owner
occupiers who live in sub-standard accommodation. In
recent years many local authorities have overspent on provision of services and have been unable to make housing
improvement grants. But certain London boroughs,
such as Westminster, are still offering help to deserving
cases. In any event, such assistance is well worth applying for, since up to 75% of all refurbishment costs are
paid in certain circumstances, and if your application
fails all you've wasted is the time taken to fill in the form.

The two main forms are mandatory and discretionary.
The former are modest amounts for bringing inadequate
houses up to reasonable standards by providing such
"standard amenities" as baths and sinks with hot and
cold water and indoor toilets. These grants have to be
awarded if the applicant's property qualifies. The only
category to fall under this heading are "intermediate
grants". Discretionary grants are awarded by councils on
the basis of need and resources. They include "repairs
grants", for pre-1919 houses needing substantial structural repairs, "improvement grants", medium sized grants
for general upgrading of poor quality homes, and
"special grants", in respect of houses in multiple occupancy. There are limits on various of the grants as regards
the rateable value of the property to be considered –
much more expensive homes will not qualify.

In general you are much more likely to receive a grant if
you live within a "Housing Action Area" or a "General
Improvement Area". These are specially designated

sections of the community which possess the highest proportion of poor housing stock in most urgent need of renovation. And you are considerably more likely to strike it rich with your grant application if you live within a rich borough. Rate-capped councils do not have discretionary grant money, and tend anyway to be run by left-wing councils which resent paying out any sums to property owners, and prefer to subsidise such do-gooders as squatters and anarchists.

Most grants require that you live in the property to be improved yourself. As a landlord who plans to let a residential property it is possible to get a grant, but you must provide a certificate stating the property is available for letting. If these conditions are breached, then the grant must be repaid. Grants become repayable at least in part if you sell the property within a certain period (normally five years) of the works being carried out. Freehold properties are preferred, but grants have been awarded to upgrade short-leasehold units on occasion. You will of course need to provide the balance of the repairs cost yourself. It has been known for developers to fix phony inflated invoices from builders to submit to the council concerned so that the householder ends up paying nothing, thanks to overestimated theoretical costs of work. Certificates of future occupation or certificates of availability for letting are required for grant monies to be paid to show you either intend to live in the property for five years or will let it for that time.

The usual rule is that a grant will be for around 50% of the total cost of works. However in General Improvement Areas grants can add up to 60% of costs, and 75% of costs in Housing Action Areas. The local town hall will have full details of any zones designated as either General Improvement or Housing Action, and will supply details of the application forms to be submitted. You should receive written approval from the council for your grant before starting works – you will have a year in which to carry them out following this permission.

Normally grant payments are made after work is finished and inspected, although in cases of hardship stage payments can be made. Cases have been known of corrupt council officials taking bribes to approve payment of grants for work never carried out – but be careful who you try this out on!

The amounts of grant monies available are changed from time to time, but maximums are between about £4,000 and £10,000 (depending on the extent of works) outside London and up to around one third more in Greater London. Clearly therefore huge developments or expensive refurbishments will not be significantly subsidised by such grants – but the sums available are not to be dismissed. It is important to plan what you are to do with the building over the next five years following improvements before accepting grants. There's little point in going through the rigmarole of applying and receiving a grant, then selling the property four years later and having to repay it all. Only apply for grants on properties which are to be a long-term home and investment, or a long-term rental investment – bearing in mind always the Rent Acts (clearly this provision excludes you letting as Holiday Lets).

Councils are loathe to make more than one grant to the same person – so make sure your best application stands a good chance of succeeding. Be prepared to wait at least a couple of months for the application to be approved following its submission. This may mean you have to wait around holding and doing no work on a semi-derelict slum property for that period until you hear the council's verdict. Some developers speed the process by putting up an "owner" to obtain a grant, and then sell the property on. If they turn your application down, you will have wasted valuable time and wasted financing charges. But in Housing Action Areas, for properties you want to live in or keep and rent – if your borough has the money to make grants – it is often worth an application. Remember they are tax-free.

28

Profiting from Enterprise Zones and the Business Expansion Scheme

Enterprise Zones are areas designated by government for special treatment in order to foster business development. Around 27 neglected inner cities and other urban black spots dotted around the UK have been selected since 1981 for favourable tax treatment. There are now almost 10,000 acres of building land in total available countrywide within Enterprise Zones. Tax incentives which encourage firms to let property in Enterprise Zones complement various tax breaks to developers of new commercial property within them.

The first attractive way a property entrepreneur can benefit is by developing industrial, office or retail premises. Such buildings qualify for 100% tax relief on purchase. Hence a developer can build units and sell them at a handsome profit to a ready pool of investors who wish to use the development as a tax shelter. Taxpayers effectively only pay £60,000 for a £100,000 building (since the 1988 budget) if they are a top rate taxpayer. The higher the marginal rate of tax for the investor – the better. The resultant yield on invested monies is therefore excellent; if net rental income on a £10,000 building is £8,000, the actual yield on invested money is 13% – a good running return, with the prospect of upwards rent reviews. And there should of course be a substantial capital gain on the sale of the property. To the extent that the tax allowance exceeds the rental income, it can be set off against an investor's other income. Technically tax payers should retain the property for 25 years to keep the full tax allowances. But there is no limit to the amount of relief which can be claimed – unlike the Business Expansion Scheme, which has a £40,000 limit per person. The relief applies only to the cost of the building – there is no relief on the cost of land. It is essential therefore to obtain certified details of the site value before purchase.

Investors can borrow the money to fund the purchase of an Enterprise Zone construction, and the interest payable on the loan qualifies for tax relief by deduction from the rental income generated. It is possible for smaller investors to club together and form a syndicate to own a single smaller warehouse or high-tech unit, say. It is of course important that the property is let to a decent tenant, to receive an income stream. Most Enterprise Zones have very generous rates holidays, normally lasting ten years. There are other incentives for prospective tenants – an exemption from industrial training levies and some industrial training board requirements, and simplification of various bureaucratic regulations and procedures. In order to encourage construction generally, there is a measure of freedom from usual local authority planning controls. Thus a developer of commercial property can offer tempting packages to tenants, find willing buyers for the completed investments, and should experience fewer problems receiving the desired planning consents, when building in Enterprise Zones.

Such areas as Corby, Dudley and Docklands have been substantially revitalised by these initiatives, and considerable numbers of new firms have moved in and created new jobs. However they have finite lives; the earliest Enterprise Zone, Clydebank, is to lose its status in 1991, while the most recent, Chatham, will cease being an Enterprise Zone in 1996. There are two such Zones in Northern Ireland – Belfast and Londonderry – and four in Wales. Offices within Enterprise Zones are mainly limited to London Docklands, but retail and light industrial or mixed user space prospects within other sites – such as Tyneside or Hartlepool – remain excellent.

Ultimately any investor in an Enterprise Zone development will face tax on his rental income under Schedule A, and ultimately capital gains tax on the eventual realisation of the property profit. However, given both the income and capital growth, even after tax a higher rate taxpayer should achieve an excellent compound return over a 25 year period, assuming the development is of a high standard and is let to quality tenants.

Several Enterprise Zone developers have clubbed together with a promoter such as Johnson Fry to launch a scheme to raise funds from the public. The developer will make both a capital profit on the construction, and quite possibly a running income for the management of the units (letting, collection of rents, maintenance etc.), which will be paid by the Trust or whatever vehicle is used for the public to invest. While the tax benefits are not available to the developer, he is sure of being able to sell on his completed development at a good profit and of a continuing management contract, which significantly cuts his risk. It should be borne in mind however that Enterprise Zones are chosen because those areas are neglected and starved of normal investment. While Britain's economy has recovered in recent years, many parts of the country still suffer a lack of tenants and business spending. Make sure any scheme you become involved in is attractive enough to overcome any such disadvantages.

The Business Expansion Scheme, or BES, is a government-sponsored tactic to boost investment in smaller companies. The 1988 budget introduced major changes to the legislation with significant implications for the property world. The BES essentially offers tax relief on any investment in a private business by an unconnected party which is left for at least five years. In the early days of the scheme many promotions were "can't fail" property development companies with high asset backing. They sucked in the majority of the money from the public going into BES, and were banned, since the scheme was designed to encourage investors to put money into riskier venture which would not attract funds otherwise and would create new jobs.

The 1988 legislation limits the amount which can be raised to £500,000, but does introduce a new form of property investment which is permissable under the BES. The current Housing Bill will create a new form of assured tenancy. This type of system will remove rent controls on residential lettings but offer tenants a degree of security of tenure. There will be various restrictions on the type and value of property which qualifies and the companies which may become involved. It is designed to encourage the generation of much more private rented accommodation, so increasing the degree of mobility possible – hence enabling people to move to where there is work. The upper limit in value of properties is £125,000 in Greater London and £85,000 in the rest of the country. Properties must be unlet when purchased. This type of scheme is attractive, since you can raise funds from friends (not relatives) who if they are top-rate (40%) taxpayers will receive £4,000 relief for every £10,000 invested. The rents can be commercial and can be in-creased within the terms of the lease. There should be both capital growth of the property purchased, and a reasonable yield from rents.

The new BES-inspired focus on assured lettings may lead to a modest reduction in residential rents, since there should be a fair number of new flats and houses to let coming onto the market. The presently desperate plight of those seeking a flat to rent without a company behind them in places like London should be eased. If the legislation works it will be a sound move, and highly profitable for those who invest in it.

29

Enfranchise Freeholds

The Leasehold Reform Act of 1967 gave householders owning a lease the right to force the landlord to sell them the freehold interest. This law creates valuable opportunities if the various conditions are met, and the marriage value of the freehold and leasehold interests is released.

The criteria are fairly strict. The leaseholder must live in the property for five years, and he must be living there when the claim is made. The house must be his only or main residence. It must be truly a house, rather than a flat. The lease owned by the occupier must be a long lease – over 21 years at original granting – and at a low rent. There are various formulas for calculating what is a low rent, depending on the area and ratable value of the house, but essentially the rent should be less than £100 a year. The lease must be within certain value limits. Most houses qualify, although exceptionally large and valuable properties will not.

If these rules can be met, then the leaseholder can force the sale of the freehold – via an intermediate leaseholder if need be. The leaseholder must give written notice to the landlord and pay a modest deposit, and prove his leasehold interest. The landlord will then indicate an acceptable price. If the price is unreasonable, the leaseholder can go to the Land Tribunal, which will make an independent ruling as to the price – which will be binding on both parties. This process does however take some time and is expensive in legal fees. It can be worthwhile agreeing a slightly higher figure than your agent will have calculated, in order to tie up a speedier deal. The leaseholder is then obliged either to pay the price as put forward by the Land Tribunal, or withdraw completely. The leaseholder will unfortunately not know how much he will have to pay until the process has gone some way down the line – incurring costs for which the leaseholder is liable.

Invariably buying the freehold as a leaseholder via enfranchisement is cheaper than buying the freehold with vacant possession. Normally the combined value of the lease and freehold bought through enfranchisement is less than the open market vacant possession freehold value of the house. But if you buy say a 10 year fag end of a 50 year lease on a house, you will have to live in it for five years before you can enfranchise. An alternative method, employed by various property wheeler-dealers, is to sign up someone to live in the property (putting it in the stooge's name and lending them the lease purchase price) and have them exercise their right after five years to enfranchise (again lending them the funds). The stooge then hands over the freehold vacant property at the agreed price – giving the stooge both cash compensation at the end of five years and free accommodation. Such an agreement has to be legally watertight and should only be undertaken with someone you trust implicitly. There might also be interesting tax implications!

Sensible freeholders will come to a compromise deal if you buy a leasehold of a house, start living there, and make it clear you intend enfranchising as soon as you can. They will forgo the possibility of you moving on within the five years for the benefit of having the money now – and perhaps more than the enfranchised freehold would normally cost. You pay a bit extra, but get the freehold immediately. Alternatively in many cases it pays the landlord to buy up the lease and marry the interests, creating a vacant freehold. In some cases freehold auction properties come up with a leaseholder who cannot afford to enfranchise. You can either come to a deal by lending them the money, and take the freehold from them after enfranchisement at an advantageous price, or you can buy the freehold and then buy up their lease. Leaseholders can ask for a 50 year extension to the lease, with an adjusted ground rent to take into account modern day values. The leaseholder can meanwhile still enfranchise, but cannot secure a second extension. Remember too that if the lease expires and the leaseholder remains in occupation, they will have conventional sitting tenant rights and can obtain a registered rent ruling.

Although not enshrined in a specific Act, sitting tenants are special purchasers normally able to buy houses – and flats – at big discounts from market prices. Normally a flat with sitting tenants will only sell for 60% of the value of the same flat vacant (excluding the capitalised value of the rent). Thus a landlord will still be making money if he sells a flat to sitting tenants at 80% of open market value. Alternatively as a sitting tenant you should be able to demand a decent cash "winkling" sum to move. If a flat is worth £100,000 vacant, and you know your landlord is in a hurry, do not accept less than £15,000 cash to move – and try for more. The game with the landlord in these situations is to judge who has more patience. Some landlords are quite happy to remain with sitting tenants, since the capital value of the property will continue to rise. Other freeholders, who have borrowed money and are paying punishing interest rates, will want to do a deal. Remember as a sitting tenant you should be able to negotiate a mortgage easily with a building society, since you'll be buying the place at much less than market value.

Be careful of tough landlords, and if you are a landlord, do not get dirty with tenants unless you are prepared to face the consequences. The Protection of Eviction Act 1977 makes it an imprisonable offence to evict or attempt to evict a sitting tenant by force. It will be in both interests to come to a peaceful cash deal – either the landlord sells to the tenant, or the landlord buys the tenant out. Both should make money (depending on how much the property owes the landlord!).

30

Raise Equity Finance

One important characteristic of property is the size of transactions – they tend to be of high value. Many individuals feel they cannot afford to undertake property deals alone, since they haven't the capital necessary, even with borrowings. One way to get around this obstacle is to syndicate such deals – in other words, involve one or more sleeping partners as equity participants. This means they contribute risk capital but do not involve themselves in the work, and they share in the ultimate profits.

Such an arrangement suits if you have just a few thousand pounds. Once you have done a couple of such deals, and given away a fair slice of the action, you may have accumulated enough profits to act alone. This type of equity finance essentially helps bridge the gap between the 66% any reasonable bank will lend on a property, and the 100% required to buy the property. Normally such passive investors will be people who know you and trust you – perhaps close friends or relatives. It is however important to only accept such contributions from those who can afford it, and those who understand there are risks to such financings. The best investors are businessmen or women who realise that venture capitalists can lose money – even in property, but who are willing to back your judgement.

It is essential to organise the partnership structure correctly. The usual system is to buy an off the shelf limited company and split the shares in the appropriate quantities. This reduces the personal liabilities for all concerned and means no-one will ever have to assume the other partners' tax debts etc., as can happen with a conventional partnership. A Board of Directors also helps a formal decision making structure work. There are frequently tax advantages to incorporation, and the sale or disposal of all or part of the business is much easier. A corporate identity is also established, which can be useful when dealing with agents, planners, and suppliers. A limited company also offers protection of the name – if it is the registered name. If you can afford "plc" status your reputation is enhanced.

A typical return for risk capital might be 50% of the profits for 100% of the equity contribution, assuming the deal doer/provider was experienced and competent. A beginner might well be expected to stump up a reasonable proportion of the money at risk – partly to show good faith. Partners should be chosen who have common aims. It is no use involving someone who will want to withdraw their cash in 9 months if the arrangement is supposed to be in place for three years. A similar attitude to risk should be adopted between partners and a joint view on the types of deals to do. If there are several investors, they should of course all be treated in a like manner. Such deals normally only function if just one developer takes control and runs the show. The sleeping partners should consider such an investment merely an adjunct to their other activities.

The simplest way to encourage backers is to ask them to guarantee up to a certain amount of bank borrowings. Depending on their creditworthiness, the bank may lend on their personal guarantee alone, or might ask them to leave a certain asset such as cash, shares or gilts as security. In some cases, a lender would take a charge over a property they owned. In each instance, the investor is able – within limits – to make use of those resources for other things, and the property partnership becomes responsible for interest. In many cases it is far less trouble to ask an investor for such a contribution rather than a cash subscription – you are therefore more likely to obtain your equity (or equivalent) finance. Such a deal also forces upon you the importance of only undertaking deals where the expected rate of return is much better than the interest received on normal bank deposits – to compensate for the inevitable risk.

It can make a lot of sense to canvas equity investment in the early days. Banks will be much keener if they see you and your partners placing a fair amount of cash on the line. Such equity finance gives you freedom to move more quickly without having to hustle around when a deal comes up trying to secure the very highest percentage of borrowings. The more equity you put down, the finer borrowing terms you can achieve. The best investors are those who will not interfere and who do not need an income from their investment. Ideally the investors should allow you to retain within the joint company the bulk of any net profits to reinvest in bigger projects. Over a period of years, the equity partners should achieve a substantial capital appreciation. The company can later be sold off in a lump or pieces – or even floated on the stock market! A distribution of profits can be made after such a liquidation.

Raising equity finance is similar in some ways to borrowing from a bank. Investors will want a clear idea of the projects you want to undertake, and rough projections of the timing, total expenditure and hoped-for proceeds. Like banks, it always pays to keep investors well informed of progress – even if there are problems to report. It is far better to alert them at an early stage to difficulties than let a crisis develop and only communicate when they have already lost money. If you are prudent however – as you must be if using other people's money (OPM) – then you ought not to go too far wrong.

One other type of equity investor is the corporate partner. In some instances they make the very best shareholders, since they can offer practical help with deals as well as money. Perhaps there is an industrial company you know whose management wish to diversify – perhaps they will back you in property and take a slice of the action. Alternatively, they might have a site which needs developing – why not offer to do it in partnership, so they share in the ultimate profits of their own land improvement. Such corporate venturers are rare beasts but worth cultivating if you find them.

Glossary

Absolute Title

The unquestionable ownership of a property. This property has a guarantee from the State that no other person has a better right to the ownership.

Architrave

A trim which masks the joint between the plaster and wood, normally found on a door or a window.

Assignment of Lease

A written document transferring all or the remainder of a lease from one person to another.

Business Tenancy

As a business tenant you are entitled to special statutory protection from the landlord in the event of an attempt to terminate the tenancy. You may apply to the courts for a new tenancy which in most cases will be granted unless the landlord can prove you have breached the original tenancy agreement (e.g. defaulted on the rent).

Blown Plaster

Plaster which has come away from the wall. This condition is usually caused by damp.

Company Letting

Many people like the added assurance of a corporate body behind the tenancy. If a landlord lets a property as a company letting, it is the company's responsibility to ensure that all inhabitants of the premises abide by the rules of the tenancy and ensure all payments of rent are met.

Conveyance

A written document transferring the ownership of land from one person to another, normally prepared by a solicitor.

Crazing

Hair cracks on the surface of concrete or cement rendering normally caused by excessive water.

Dry Rot

A condition affecting timber whereby fungi feeding on dampness cause the timber to decay. Dry rot is difficult to remove completely without burning the infected wood, and fungi has even been known to transmit moisture through brickwork.

Easements

Various rights held by an owner with regard to his neighbours' property. For example a person may be refused planning permission to increase the height of a garden shed if it obstructs his neighbour's natural light (easement of light).

Endowment Property

A property that is permanently owned by a charity.

Enforcement Notice

This notice is issued by the local planning authority in the event of an alleged breach of planning control. It lists steps which should be taken within a specified time period to rectify the breach.

Enfranchisement of Residential Freeholds

The process whereby a leaseholder can force the sale of the freehold of a house providing a certain number of criteria are met, e.g. the lease must have more than 21 years left to run, the house must have been the principle private residence for the last five years.

Exchange of Contracts

The time at which parties are legally committed to proceed with the sale/purchase of a property. A deposit of approximately 10% of the purchase price is normally paid to the vendor's solicitor, with a date for completion mutually agreed.

Fee Simple

The absolute ownership of a property which will not end upon death or the occurrence of any other event.

Gentrification of an Area

The process of change in an area whereby relatively poor but cheaper housing is purchased and improved, then is sold off at a profit to those who would prefer to live in an area nearby but can't quite afford it. These people may bring new money into the area, encouraging the opening of new service industries (restaurants, wine bars etc.) which in turn encourage more middle class people into the area.

Harassment of Occupier

A landlord is not permitted to threaten a tenant with violence or other pressure in order to reposses the property. Failure to observe the correct procedures evicting a tenant may result in legal action.

Joist

A large beam, either wooden or steel, which directly supports the floor. The span of a wooden joist is normally 5 metres, but this length can be extended at an extra cost.

Land Certificate

Land must be registered. The Land Certificate is the document issued by the Land Registry to the owner of the land as proof of that ownership.

Letting Agent

A person who acts on behalf of landlords, finding suitable tenants for flats and houses. In many cases the letting agent will also undertake to manage the property, i.e. deal with the tenants' complaints. Their fee is paid by the landlord.

Local Searches

The forms sent to the local authorities, normally by the purchaser's solicitor. Certificates would be sent back detailing plans affecting properties in the specified area.

Maintenance Period

The period of time after the completion of a contract during which the contractor is liable to rectify at his own expense any faults which occur in the work just carried out.

MIRAS

This stands for "Mortgage Interest Relief At Source" and is the most common way for a person to receive the statutory governmental mortgage tax relief.

Protimeter

An instrument used by a surveyor to test an area for damp.

Qualified Title

A guarantee of good title subject to a qualification in the Land Register. This guarantee of ownership does not protect the owner in respect of a specified qualification.

Quiet Enjoyment

A tenant is entitled to possess and enjoy the land he has leased without unwarranted interference from the landlord. This is taken to be the case in every lease unless specifically excluded.

Rack Rent

The total annual sum of rent that a tenant could reasonably expect to pay on the open market.

Restrictive Covenants

Covenants in a lease which prevent certain activities from taking place on the premises e.g. may not be permitted to serve food.

Retention Money

On completion of a contract the contractor will be paid his fee less a percentage of the agreed sum. This percentage, called the retention money, will be paid at the end of the maintenance period when the owner of the building and his consultants are satisfied that the contractor has fulfilled his obligations.

Reversionary Leasehold

A leasehold with only a few years remaining before it reverts back to the freeholder. The freeholder may feel that in certain circumstances, e.g. varying time periods left on each unit making up the freehold, it would be more profitable to sell an extension of the lease.

Roof Flashing

Metal, normally lead or zinc, that excludes water from junctions between the roof covering and another surface.

Security of Tenure

The statutory protection given to tenants that restricts a landlord's rights to obtain possession. Conditions vary according to tenancy, but a landlord may have to seek a court order to evict the tenant.

Service Charge

A fee levied on a leaseholder by the freeholder for the upkeep of the building and any services provided. Mainly applicable to blocks of flats or converted houses. Fee may be for a variety of "services" – anything from the employment of a caretaker to the upkeep and well-being of the communal potted plants. May also vary dramatically from one year to the next depending on the amount of major works carried out (e.g. roof re-slating).

Stakeholder's Deposit

A nominal proportion of the total cost of a property for sale paid by the purchaser as a gesture of goodwill to prove to the vendor that he is a serious buyer. A purchaser does not legally have to part with any money until the exchange of contracts, but may wish to do so if it will persuade the vendor not to remarket the property.

Stamp Duty

Governmental Tax payable on certain legal documents including the sale/purchase of a property. Currently levied at 1% of the value of the property.

Title Deeds

Documents proving ownership of a property and the terms under which it is owned.

Valuation Survey

A structural survey carried out on behalf of the purchaser's building society or bank, the purpose being to ascertain the mortgagability of the property. A purchaser should have an independent survey done in addition to the valuation survey because although the property may be mortgagable it does not necessarily mean it has no structural defects. Both the valuation survey and the independent survey are paid for by the purchaser.

Winkling

The extraction of sitting tenants from residential property by professional developers through persuasion, bribery or coertion.

Wayleave

The permission given to pass over land e.g. British Gas
may be given permission to lay pipes on land not owned
by the company.

Bibliography/Further Reading

London Property Guide, edited by Carrie Segrave, published by Mitchell Beazley, 1988, £9.95.

Surveying for Home-Buyers, by David Broughton and John Dryborough, published by Penguin, 1983, £1.50.

A Layman's Guide to Profitable Letting, by Robert B. Davies, published by Jofleur Publications, 1986, £4.95.

The Valuation of Property Investments, by Nigel Enever, published by The Estates Gazette, 1977, £4.60.

The Complete Real Estate Advisor, by Daniel J. deBenedictis, published by Fireside Books, 1983, $8.95.

Running Your Own Building Business, by Kim Ludman, published by Kogan Page, 1985, £4.95.

Do-It-Yourself Conveyancing, by J. C. Potter, published by Prism Press, 1988, £7.95.

Property Renovation Profits, by Chartsearch Limited, 1987, £12.00.

Understanding Property Law, by W. T. Murphy & Simon Roberts, published by Fontana, 1987, £4.95.

Property Auctions, edited by Clive Carpenter & Susan Harris, published by Estates Gazette, 1988, £13.00.

Housing, Tenancy, and Planning Law, by A. J. Lomnicki, published by Heinemann/Made Simple, 1981, £2.95.

How to Buy and Renovate a Cottage, by Stuart Turner, published by Kogan Page, 1987, £6.95.

Guide to Domestic Building Surveys, by Jack Bowyer, published by The Architectural Press, 1977, £3.50.

How I Turned $1,000 into Five Million in Real Estate, by William Nickerson, published by Simon & Schuster, 1980, $19.95.

The National Association of Estate Agents Year Book,

published by Cornhill Publications Limited, 1987, £15.00.

The Penguin Dictionary of Building, by John S. Scott, published by Penguin, 1984, £4.95.

Rachman and Who Owns London?, both by Shirley Green, published by Weidenfeld & Nicolson.

The Two Tycoons, by Charles Gordon, published by Hamish Hamilton, 1984, £9.95.

Land Law Notebook, by Paul Barber, published by Butterworths.

Buying and Selling a House or Flat, by Majorie Giles, published by Pan, 1981, £1.75.

The Concise Dictionary of Law, Oxford University Press, 1983, £4.95.

The Streetwise Guide to Buying and Selling Your Home, by Martin Village, published by Piatkus, 1987, £3.95.

Law Made Simple, by Padfield & Barker, published by Heinemann, 1985, £3.95.

How to Buy a House, Condo, Or Co-Op, by Michael Thomsett, published by Consumer Reports Books, 1987, $9.00.

The Homeowner's Guide to the Law, Cedric Meadow-croft, published by Fourmat Publishing, 1987, £6.95.

The New Investor's Guide to Making Money in Real Estate by Walter Stern, published by Grosset & Dunlap, 1976, $4.95.

The Property Boom, by Oliver Marriot, published by Hamish Hamilton, 1967.

The major weekly trade magazine is The Estates Gazette, priced 60p, available from good newsagents. There are also Estates Times and Chartered Surveyor Weekly, as well as various building trade journals. Essentially the only good newsletter is Property Confidential, published monthly.